LIVE
YOUR STORY

WALKING OUT YOUR **IDENTITY**
AND **PURPOSE**
WITH THE **MASTER** STORYTELLER

STEPHANIE N. HALL

LIVE YOUR STORY
WALKING OUT YOUR **IDENTITY** AND **PURPOSE** WITH THE **MASTER** STORYTELLER

Author Photo by Kaitlyn Hickey
Cover and Interior Page design by True Potential, Inc.

ISBN: 978-1-943852-28-4 (paperback)
ISBN: 978-1-943852-29-1 (ebook)

Library of Congress Control Number: 2016950017

True Potential
REACH THE WORLD

True Potential, Inc.
PO Box 904, Travelers Rest, SC 29690
www.truepotentialmedia.com

Printed in the United States of America.

To Mom, Dad, and J. (and family) —
Thank you for always being my best friends and biggest fans!
I wouldn't be me without you!
I love you and am so grateful for each of you.

CONTENTS

PART III: INTENTION

PART IV: INTEGRATION

ACKNOWLEDGMENTS

When a book is written, far more people are involved than the one with his or her name on the cover. This book is no different, and I want to thank others who have played a part in the process.

Thanks to my parents for their support and belief in me, for reading drafts, and for listening to me talk about this book for the past seven years! Thanks to Liz, Libby, Debbie, Katie, Patty, Luke, and Chris for reading portions and drafts over the years and giving me feedback and encouragement. Thank you to James Rovira for editing assistance and to Christy Kessler for her significant input in making this book better. Thanks to Kaitlyn Hickey who donated her time and talent to provide the photo for the back cover. Thank you to those who let me share their stories. Thank you to the people who have contributed financially to the publishing process and to my life and ministry over the past fifteen years. Thank you to the many friends who have supported me through prayer during this process. Thank you to Steve Spillman and the people at True Potential for working with me to get this message out, and to Chris Maxwell for connecting me with him. Finally, many humble thanks to those of you who have purchased and read this book. I am honored that you have allowed me to share my story with you, and I would love to hear your stories as well. Please visit my website at www.stephanienhall.com or email me at steph@stephanienhall.com.

INTRODUCTION

I used to dream of writing a book. I had notebooks full of character names and ideas for plots, but it never got any further than that. It just never seemed to go anywhere. I suppose it's because I got bored and gave up. Perhaps, for right now, I'm not meant to be the writer of new stories but simply a teller of those already written. The stories in this book are written by the Master Storyteller. There have been people — myself included — who have tossed in their own thoughts here and there; maybe they even changed the original story a bit, but the Master is just that — a Master of taking our stories and making them His own once again.

My story is normal, whatever that is. There is nothing particularly spectacular about it other than its Author and the things He has taught me through my process of living it. It has not always been an easy story to live in, but every fairytale princess does her time locked in a tower or cleaning the fireplace until, at last, her true identity is discovered, and the Prince rescues her. I am being dramatic here, of course. There was no tower or fireplace in my story, but... You'll see.

My hope is that by sharing my journey of becoming the person I am today, others will recognize their own paths to discovering why they are on this little planet. There are many voices these days telling us how we should look, who we should be, and what the meaning of life is — if there even is one. There are whole generations searching for acceptance and significance, and I hope that by being open with my own process of discovery, I can help others find the fulfillment of those needs.

Before I start to describe this book and its purpose, I want to add a note about this search for acceptance and significance. While I believe the desire to know our identity and purpose is universal, that doesn't mean each of us must have an "identity crisis." According to one common definition, an "identity crisis" is "a period of psychological distress... when a person is seeking a clearer sense of self and an acceptable role in society." I think we all go through the process of seeking that sense of who we are and our place in the world, but I do not believe it has to include "psychological distress." My prayer is that God will guide each of us into more of His original design for us as we trust and rest in Him.

The premise of this book is that as we seek to answer the question, "Who am I?" a number of components are necessary, and with the combination of them all, there is exponential growth in the power of walking out our identity and purpose. Four I's are crucial in reaching our full potential. They are covered in the four parts of this book: Intimacy, Identity, Intention, and Integration.

The first part of this book is about intimacy with God and my experience of knowing and being known by Him. That might seem an odd place to start a book about discovering our identity and purpose, but I discovered an interesting thing about the word "identity." If you look up "identity" in a thesaurus, you'll find contradictory words used to describe it, such as uniqueness and sameness, for example. Uniqueness is understandable; after all, we are all different and have our own identity that has been designed and built into us by God.

As I thought more about it, though, sameness also makes sense. Identity comes from the same root word as identical. Finding ourselves doesn't mean deciding who we want to become. This process is really all about finding out who we already are and walking in that knowledge with complete confidence and freedom. We are on a journey to become identical to the original design given to us by the Master Storyteller. To do that, we must first know the One Who designed us in His own image. That is the reason we start with intimacy. I am convinced our identity and purpose can be found fully only as we search in the light of our relationship with God.

As we look at our intimacy with God, we'll explore a number of different relationships we can have with Him during our journey. While words like "stage" or "level" are used to describe these different relationships and the degree of intimacy they suggest, it is important to keep in mind no one relationship is more important or more holy than another. I think of these stages as a continuum on which we will likely move back and forth throughout our journey with God. Here is a table to outline the stages of relationship and levels of intimacy we will cover. This is not an exhaustive list, and you may be aware of others, but these are the levels of relationship I have experienced in my own journey so far. We will look at each of these levels individually because each is significant to who we are.

Stage/Level	Attribute(s) of this relational stage
Creator/Creation	Individual may or may not acknowledge God's existence or place in his/her life.
Savior/Sinner	Individual recognizes his/her need for a Savior and is surrendered to God.
Shepherd/Sheep	Individual is dependent on God for guidance, protection, and provision, and he/she recognizes God's voice.
Master/Servant	Individual seeks to hear and obey God and serve Him with his/her life.
Friends	Individual recognizes God as a friend and communication is open and two-way.
Father/Child	Individual recognizes God as a loving Father who protects, disciplines, guides, gives good gifts, speaks destiny and blessing, and gives an inheritance.
Lover/Beloved	Individual recognizes his/her place as part of the Bride of Christ, and therefore His Beloved. Individual responds with love toward the Lover.

As we move into Part Two: Identity, I'll share more in depth about my own story. The best way to share all I've learned about discovering who God created you to be is to bring you along on my own journey, though I'm still learning exactly who I am. In the midst of these chapters chronicling my life so far, I will reference many passages from J.R.R. Tolkien's *Lord of the Rings* trilogy. There will be references to other movies and books throughout this book, but God has used *Lord of the Rings* in particular to speak volumes to me about my own story. If you've never seen or read the story, I suggest at least watching the movies before you embark on Part Two.

In Part Three: Intention, I focus on discovering the intentions God had when he created us. This section covers several topics I have found essential to knowing my purpose. I hope to give enough of an understanding of each of the topics, so you can see how they fit into the framework of discovering why God put you on the Earth "for such a time as this." I also share stories from the Bible to illustrate the principles highlighted throughout the book.

Finally, in Part Four: Integration, I discuss the need for godly community and how important it is to be integrated into the Body of Christ. I then bring everything together to help you see how all of these components fit together in your own story.

One more note about the book before we begin: I recommend answering all the questions at the end of each chapter. I also propose films, books, activities, and/or music for each chapter for those who would like to experience the stories that have impacted me. Those are optional. The questions, however, I strongly urge you to answer because they will allow you to see how the principles I'm learning in my own story can apply to yours.

Discuss these questions with a friend or small group. Journal about them or write a short answer in the space provided, write a song, or keep your thoughts in your head. It doesn't matter how you process the information, but it does matter that you take time to do it. Otherwise, reading this book will only be, at best, a nice story.

CHAPTER ONE

THE JOURNEY BEGINS

"It's a dangerous business going out of your door. You step into the Road, and if you don't keep your feet, there is no telling where you might be swept off to." – J.R.R. Tolkien, *The Fellowship of the Ring*

In order to share with you what I have learned over the course of my life, I must share my life. Before we delve into the topic of intimacy with God, I introduce you to the girl who started this journey. The girl described in this chapter knew nothing of what comes in the following chapters. She was often lost and had no clue how to find her next step toward all that God had planned for her. This chapter is my story, or at least the beginning of it.

We all have testimonies of what God has done in our lives. Some stories may seem more intense, but none are boring. My story may lack drugs, alcohol, jail, or any of the many visible conditions from which people have been rescued, but that does not mean it is better or worse. God has rescued me from the lies of the Enemy and from myself. I hope my story brings you encouragement.

I was born in Orlando, Florida, in July 1980. I had a family that was as near perfect as any I have seen. My brother, J., is two years older than I am and was my best friend for most of my childhood. My parents decided to homeschool us when J. was entering 2nd grade and I was in kindergarten. I am very thankful for their decision and willingness to sacrifice the time they could have spent on other things while we were in school. For much of my childhood, my parents worked and arranged their schedules so one of them could be with us and oversee our schoolwork. They also organized a homeschool group that engaged in field trips, science fairs, track and field days, and other activities.

I had a fantastic childhood filled with family vacations to civil war sites, camping trips, visits to Disney World during the years my dad worked there, opportunities to learn to play the guitar and piano, mission trips, and more. I had so much fun with my family and friends. I loved hanging out with J., who was my hero.

> As I grew up in this seemingly perfect environment, I began to struggle with who I was. I couldn't put it into words then, but I was wrestling to find my identity.

As I grew up in this seemingly perfect environment, I began to struggle with who I was. I couldn't put it into words then, but I was wrestling to find my identity. I idolized J., and never felt I measured up to him.

Growing up, I was allowed less freedom than J., partly because he was older and largely because I was a girl. I grew to hate being a girl; it limited my freedom. Everything was regarded as more dangerous for me. It didn't matter that I was as strong as most boys my age; I was judged an easier target for adults who prey on children. When I hit my preteen years, I became a feminist — not in pursuing justice and equality, but in resenting men and making it known I didn't need them. I became offended if a guy offered to help me carry something. After all, I could bench press 115 lbs., so why would I need his help? I hated having doors opened for me. I was definitely independent when it came to physical tasks because I wanted to prove I was just as strong and tough as the boys.

While growing up and being the social butterfly that I was, I had many friends in addition to my big brother. Over the years, though, I realized all my best girlfriends liked J. Well, everyone liked him, but they *liked* him. The thought began to cross my mind they were my friends only to get closer to him, perhaps. Would we be friends otherwise? My self-esteem began to take shape, and it was not pretty. I tried very hard to be the best I could be, but it wasn't working. Today, I realize my problem was not trying to be the best *me;* I was trying to be the best version of J. I could be — and of course, failing miserably.

It is sometimes scary to clearly see what hides just below the surface. No one who knew me would ever have guessed I felt these things. I didn't recognize the feelings myself until much later in life. At church I was known as a good, responsible girl, the kind who all the mothers wanted to have babysit their children and even wanted their daughters to grow up to be. It seemed to me many thought I was as near to perfect as a girl could be. Little did they know... Little did I know!

In my senior year of high school, my emotions and self-doubt stirred under the surface. They became tumultuous waves I thought would drown me. I was strong enough — or perhaps weak enough — to keep everything hidden from others, but I soon became acutely aware of the feelings of insignificance and even invisibility that had been growing in me.

Several different winds blew simultaneously to create the perfect storm. I began a dual enrollment program at the local community college and was in a classroom setting on a regular basis for the first time in my academic career. Furthermore, I had two of J.'s former teachers, and he was a straight-A student. I was also just getting accustomed to driving, which scared me for reasons I can't explain.

Rich Mullins, a musician I met when I was a teenager, had died in a car accident. I don't understand why his death impacted me so strongly, but I didn't eat for a week. I'd met him briefly only once, but I felt as though I'd lost someone very close to me.

The strongest wind in my perfect storm was J. moving to Colorado to train with a missions and outreach organization. My lifelong best friend was now two thousand miles away. I was left behind. I felt I had somehow disappeared. Of course, as usual, my best friend *liked* J., so when we got together or spoke on the phone, we talked about how much she missed him. At church, where people used to say, "Hello. How are you?" it became, "Hi. Have you heard from J. lately?"

However, the largest gale came at home. My parents missed J. like crazy. We all did. But as the holidays approached — the first without the whole family together — my parents decided on no Christmas tree. It simply didn't feel like Christmas without everyone together. As silly as it sounds now, my seventeen-year-old brain was telling me, "You are not enough. You alone are not worth celebrating the holidays with as we normally would."

The thoughts and feelings of inferiority that had been hiding under the surface for many years were suddenly exposed in my conscious mind for the first time. For a period of almost nine months, I contemplated disappearing. Not running away, but going to heaven. My brain told me no one would notice if I wasn't around. I thought about stepping in front of a bus, but I wondered if suicide was a sure ticket to hell. After all, you couldn't ask for forgiveness afterward if it worked.

However, it wasn't just the fear of hell that kept me alive and out of the way of moving vehicles. Deep down, I knew I would be missed. I couldn't put my family through the pain of loss. Even if I hadn't felt like anyone knew I existed, I knew the sudden loss would bring them pain. I couldn't cause pain. They already missed J., and he was only in Colorado and would come back to visit.

I'm not exactly sure what eventually snapped me out of that very dark time in my life. Whatever it was, I know God was a large part of it. I also remember a few people who were involved in that process. One youth worker at my church gave me a little 12-inch Christmas tree, with all the trimmings, to show me celebrating that year with me was still worth someone's time. God sent people just when I needed them, and He sustained me through that time, even when I wasn't aware of His presence and work in my life.

As the months and years went on, I continued to work hard to be the best me I could be, not realizing I still didn't know who that was. I was whatever I was doing. I was a homeschooler — and proud of it! I was a babysitter. I was a worship leader at church. I was a piano teacher. I was a nursing student. I was on my way to being a missionary nurse. Am I the only one who ever confused identity with actions?

In April 2001, I graduated nursing school with my Associate Degree in Nursing. I was a straight-A student, second in my class. I aced my licensure exam. I thought I had self-esteem, but I had accomplishment-esteem. I had lived up to J.'s example and even surpassed it by getting a degree. I had dreamed of being a missionary since my first mission trip at the age of 13, and now my training and education would open doors for me to go to nearly any nation in the world!

> As the months and years went on, I continued to work hard to be the best me I could be, not realizing I still didn't know who that was.

In June 2001, just before my 21st birthday, my parents and I moved to Colorado to join the organization where J. now worked. Once again, the family was together, and we even had a new member. My brother had married in March of that year, so I had a new sister to get to know.

In September, I started a missions training course, the next step toward my dream of serving as a missionary. As much as I enjoyed learning more about God and sharing Him with others during those few months, I became aware of a crisis in my heart and mind. For eight years, my goals had been unwavering: get a nursing degree and complete a training course to be a missionary. I never thought beyond the training aspects of my plan, so as I neared the end of the training phase, I began to panic. What do I do now? This has been my life's goal, and now I don't know where to go. I'm so glad God sees what's ahead on the path because I tend to get tunnel vision and then panic when the tunnel opens up to new horizons and options I've never before dreamed.

After completing the first training course, I participated in a secondary training focused on strategies to live and minister in "creative access countries." Since then, I have been on staff with an outreach organization and have continued to live my dream. Because I've learned so much, I've been ruined for the ordinary — once a person has experienced extraordinary things with God, even seemingly ordinary moments can brim with the possibilities of the extraordinary.

In the years since becoming a missionary, I have been through training and have helped train others. I lived in Afghanistan for almost two years, working with a community health education project and overseeing women's literacy classes. I have been to approximately thirty countries and have had opportunities to use my various skills in ways I never dreamed I could — singing on live radio, cooking for dozens of people, translating Bible stories for women to practice reading, and so many other opportunities. I have been to many places, tasted exotic flavors, met different people, and experienced unusual things, which I hope are only the beginning experiences of what our God has created.

I will share more of my story in Part Two: Identity. For now, you have enough of my background to delve more deeply into the things I have learned in the years since I started my adventure with God. Things like going deeper in intimacy with God, identity and purpose, and why exactly those are so important. I wouldn't be who I am today without the experiences described in this chapter, but moving on from here is where the story really gets good!

QUESTIONS TO PONDER:

1. Do you identify with any parts of my story? Which ones?

_____

_____

_____

_____

_____

_____

2. What did you feel while reading my story? Why?

_____

_____

_____

_____

_____

_____

RECOMMENDED ACTIVITIES:

1. Write out your story and see what God reveals to you about it.

_____

_____

_____

_____

_____

_____

_____

Part I: Intimacy

"It is only in God that we discover our origin, our identity, our meaning, our purpose, our significance, and our destiny. Every other path leads to a dead end." – Rick Warren, *The Purpose Driven Life: What On Earth Am I Here For?*

CHAPTER TWO

IN THE BEGINNING

"In the beginning God created..." – Genesis 1:1[1]

Several years ago, when I first heard God asking me to write a book, the end product looked much differently than what you're holding right now. The material for the first section of the book didn't even exist yet. Once I started writing, however, I realized I couldn't proceed with the topic of finding your identity and purpose without first laying some groundwork.

Many people believe they have "found themselves" and are very successful in their careers despite having no belief in God. Yet I venture to guess that because of those beliefs, they are not reaching their

---

1   Unless otherwise noted, all scripture quotations are from the *New American Standard Version* of the Bible (NASB)

potential or fulfilling the purpose God intended for them when He designed them. Although they may seem happy, or even truly be happy, I bet if success left them behind, their identity, purpose, and self-worth would quickly follow in its wake.

It is only in the light of our relationship with God that we are able to fully see who we are meant to be and why. After all, who better to guide us to our design than the One who designed us?

There are many relationships we have with God during the course of our journey through life. He is our Healer, Comforter, Guide, Prince of Peace, Counselor, and so much more! You'll notice none of those things listed are in the table in the introduction to this book. The reason is, just as a parent or friend can fill many roles in our lives while remaining our parent or friend, these are roles God fills within our relationship with Him. He may use other people at times to fill these roles, but He is always the One who provides the avenue for our needs to be met.

Some roles, however, can be associated with a certain level of intimacy. As we flesh out Who God is and how we relate to Him, I will explore some of these levels. Not every person will necessarily go through every stage, and maybe you're aware of some that I don't cover. These are simply the levels of intimacy I have experienced in my own relationship with God so far.

As we begin looking at these stages or levels of intimacy with God, I want to say again that relationship with Him is not necessarily a linear progression. It is more of a continuum or a spectrum on which we move back and forth. Aside from the first stage,[2] no place on the spectrum is more or less connected to God. Just because someone

---

2   It is possible for one to be at the first point on the continuum –
     Creator/creation – and not have a relationship with God. Once a
     person has moved beyond the Creator/creation stage of relation-
     ship, while still impacted at times with the revelation of the Creator
     and the majesty of His creations, the relationship between God and
     that person will always be marked by another of the stages as well.
     Because of this dynamic, one who is at the first stage can be less
     connected to God.

else is enjoying the place of feeling like a "child" of God doesn't mean he or she is more spiritual or any more valuable than a "sheep." During our individual journeys with our God, we will visit most of these stages repeatedly. As much as I would love to feel like the "beloved" of God every day forever, I'm afraid that's not how relationships work, and this one is no different.

Creator & Creation

The first important point to this relationship is that truth exists and is absolute. I know many people today say truth is relative and what's true for me may not be true for everyone else. I'm sorry, but that's rubbish! Truth is truth, whether or not we believe it. It is always true that murder and theft are wrong. It is also true that everyone on the planet is in relationship *to* God, though not all may have a relationship *with* Him. Even people who don't believe in Him are at a place on the continuum, which consists of being the creation of a loving Creator. People can deny this fact all they want, but the truth is God designed each one of us and knit us together according to His design.

> I know many people today say truth is relative and what's true for me may not be true for everyone else. I'm sorry, but that's rubbish! Truth is truth, whether or not we believe it.

One of my favorite experiences of nursing school was learning about the intricacies of the human body and how it works. It always blew my mind to think one malfunction of a cell here or there could cause havoc throughout the whole body. God thought through every detail, and those details will never cease to amaze me. I'm always confounded by how some people find it easy to believe that level of detail and perfection in design just happened accidentally. Call me crazy, but to believe everything in creation happened on its own takes more faith than believing in the presence and power of a Creator.

Savior & Sinner, Saved by Grace

Whatever your beliefs on the matter, you are the creation of a loving God, and that will not change. Once you accept that truth, the jump to the next stage — Savior and sinner — isn't a huge leap. I know "sin" is a word that gets thrown around a lot, but it isn't often defined these days. Allow me to share my definition: sin is anything done out of selfishness and outside the boundaries God established for us. Knowing my tendency to act selfishly and stepping outside those limits myself, when confronted with an all-powerful, all-knowing Creator, my natural reaction is to feel small, inadequate, and unworthy to be in relationship with Him.

In reality, all of those shortcomings are true of all of us — we are selfish, inadequate and unworthy — as long as we are standing on our own works. Sinful man cannot stand in the presence of a holy God. All of us fall short of the standard of perfection that the holiness of God requires of us. Thankfully, the story doesn't end here. God loves us despite all of the mistakes and willful choices we have made that separate us from His presence. Because of that love, He provided a way for us to stand before Him clothed in the righteousness of Christ instead of our own dirty rags.

The Problem

Before we talk about God's way of fixing the problem that separates us from Him, we need to address briefly the problem. Many people in the Church today like to point out the sins of others. We talk about murder (whether of those born already or those hidden inside their mother's womb), theft, lying, sexual sin (any sexual act outside the boundaries set by the Creator), and others. Unfortunately, in our zeal to uphold so many ideals of our loving God, we often skim past the commandments not to judge others and to avoid gossip.

Yes, we who follow Christ are far from perfect. In fact, I find myself often falling for the very first human sin ever committed: doubting the character of God. That one action led to everything that has ever separated man from the love of his Creator. I suppose every person on the planet has fallen prey to this temptation since its first successful use on Adam and Eve in the Garden of Eden.

In Genesis 3:1 the serpent simply asked Eve, "Did God really say…?" (NIV). Eve answered with her husband's restatement of God's words. The serpent was able to counter with a clever temptation, suggesting Eve believe God was holding out on her and Adam. They experienced a moment of doubt in the goodness of God, and sin entered the world.

This doubt in God's character is still the root of every wrong act committed today. The limits or laws God has asked us to live by are a loving boundary established in His wisdom to keep us from hurting ourselves and others. He isn't a killjoy who is out to suck the fun and life out of living. Instead, He is the Source of life and pleasure. He created everything that is pleasurable, and He is the One who knows best how life and its pleasures are good for us. That is why He set up boundaries for us to live within. Moving outside those limits is necessary or desirable only if we doubt His character and believe He is holding out on us.

The Answer

Now that we've identified the problem, let's talk about the solution: Jesus Christ. God's own Son came and lived the perfect life that we never could. Then He chose to endure torture and death on the cross, defeated the powers of hell and death, and rose again to life. His victory had major effects. We discuss one of them more in depth in the third part of this book. But one in particular is important at this point: Jesus Christ's victory over sin and death unlocks the door for us to move forward in relationship with God. We can, therefore, move on the relationship spectrum from Creator and creation to Savior and sinner-saved-by-grace.

Although Jesus did all the work to unlock the door, it is up to us to walk through it. It can be difficult for some of us to take that step through the door. The first challenge is recognizing our own sin. Once we acknowledge our sin, an entirely new batch of struggles comes with that knowledge. Oddly enough, when I find myself facing my own wrongdoings, the two challenges I experience most often seem to contradict each other. The two challenges are: 1) admitting and owning my sin and 2) letting it be washed away.

First, when turning away from any wrongdoing, it is important to confess. Own your sin and apologize, instead of making excuses or blaming circumstances and other people. I don't like taking responsibility for my wrongs, whether in front of other people or between God and me. No one enjoys making mistakes, and most people like it even less when they have to admit it. The blame game has been ongoing since sin first entered the world with Adam and Eve, and it continues today. It is uncomfortable to take responsibility, but necessary if we're going to truly deal with our sin.

Although once my mind has owned the sin, it's usually hesitant to let it go. Often it seems no matter how much I confess and allow God to forgive and forget, my mind refuses to forget. Instead, it holds onto a running tab of my failures, using them as an arsenal to bring shame and guilt whenever the opportunity presents itself.

> First, when turning away from any wrongdoing, it is important to confess. Own your sin and apologize, instead of making excuses or blaming circumstances and other people.

My mind isn't alone in its record keeping, either. I mentioned the serpent when discussing Adam and Eve's first encounter with the temptation to go against God's words. That serpent has gone by many names in the millennia since then: Satan, Lucifer, the Devil, Father of Lies, the Enemy, and many others. Whatever we call him, we must realize he is still a player in the story of our lives. One of his favorite roles to play, besides tempter, is accuser. He loves bringing up our past hurts and failings to remind us how unworthy we are of God's Love.

We can never forget that our heart has an enemy that is desperate to keep us from moving closer in intimacy to our Creator. Satan would love to keep us from believing a Creator even exists. If we persist in believing in God's existence, though, the next recourse is to make us believe He is an angry, lightning bolt hurler from whom we should steer away. Satan accuses and reminds us of our failures to make us believe this All-Powerful Being will never love us and accept us as His own.

Romans 5:8 states, "But God demonstrates His own love toward us, in that while we were yet sinners, Christ died for us." When we realize the truth that God loves us and accepts us as we are, it frees us to accept the love and forgiveness we are offered, by grace, through Christ, no matter what our accuser is whispering in our ears. Only then can we begin to listen for a very different voice. In the next chapter, we explore the process of learning to hear and recognize the voice of our Shepherd.

QUESTIONS TO PONDER:

1. What do you believe about the beginning of creation? How did everything get here?

_____

_____

_____

_____

_____

2. Have you accepted the forgiveness of God and allowed Him to save you through His grace?

_____

_____

_____

_____

RECOMMENDED READING

1. Genesis 1–3

_____

_____

RECOMMENDED ACTIVITIES:

2. If you have never moved into a relationship with God as your Savior, I encourage you to find someone who can introduce you to Him and help you enter into that relationship.

_____

_____

LIVE
CHAPTER THREE

HE SAID WHAT?

"The skies were made by GOD's command; he breathed the word and the stars popped out." – Psalm 33:6 (The Message)

Shepherd & Sheep

Shepherds are mentioned often in the Bible. God chose the shepherd David to rule His people. He chose shepherds to be the first to share the good news of Christ's birth. They were likely considered the lowest rung on the Israelite job ladder, and yet God not only chose them for big jobs repeatedly, but also He chose to equate Himself with them. References to God shepherding His people abound throughout the Bible — from Genesis to Revelation.

Knowing God as our Shepherd makes us His sheep. Here's what I know about sheep: Sheep are not the smartest animals in the world. They follow one another blindly and must be led to food and water sources by someone who cares for them. They are completely help-less on their own. They need provision and protection given by a shepherd. I don't know about you, but I don't find this comparison a particularly flattering one. And yet, it is accurate.

I am a sheep in need of a Good Shepherd, and thankfully, God is the best! The aspect I most enjoy about the sheep/Shepherd relationship is we can know His voice. One of my favorite Bible passages regarding sheep is John 10:2–5, 27. It states,

"But he who enters by the door is a shepherd of the sheep. To him the doorkeeper opens, and the sheep hear his voice, and he calls his own sheep by name and leads them out. When he puts forth all his own, he goes ahead of them, and the sheep follow him because they know his voice. A stranger they simply will not follow but will flee from him because they do not know the voice of strangers…My sheep hear My voice, and I know them, and they follow Me."

Our ability to hear and recognize the voice of our Shepherd is foundational to much of our journey with Him.

We are His sheep and He wants us to know His voice. I know fellow Christians who think God stopped speaking because He spoke to enough people ages ago, so we could later have a book to read all abou it. I love the Bible, and I am very thankful we have it as a tool to learn about God by His own words. I believe, however, He wants to communicate more to His people!

Not only are we sheep in need of recognizing His voice, but also all subsequent stages of relationship require us to know His voice. Our ability to hear and recognize the voice of our Shepherd is foundational to much of our journey with Him.

Learning to Hear His Voice

When I first started learning about hearing God's voice, I felt frustrated most of the time. It seemed everyone around me was hearing cool stuff, but I didn't hear anything. It took me a long time to realize this is a process that takes practice. As I have walked alongside others in this process, more than one has come to me in tears, thinking they must be doing something wrong or must not be close enough to God because they aren't hearing anything. When this happens, I share with them the verse God used to encourage me. Psalm 46:10 states, "Cease striving and know that I am God; I will be exalted among the nations, I will be exalted in the earth."

Some Bible translations say "be still and know…," but I don't want to equate being still with sitting around doing nothing. The words "cease striving" speak something completely different to me, and I love the idea that I just have to stop trying so hard. Even after years of practice, I can get so overly focused on thinking I should be hearing something or thinking I've missed something that I can't hear anything. My focus is on me and not on the One I'm supposed to be listening to, and that's never an effective way to hear anyone.

The following principles are the steps I learned when I first started listening for God's voice.[3] Our God, being Who He is, doesn't speak in the same way every time, so I have found these principles to be a good starting point if you're not used to hearing Him.

1. Thank God for Who He is and that He wants to talk to you. Be specific about His character and the attributes you're thankful for. This is a great way to focus on Him and get your mind in a place that is open to Him.

2. Ask Him to search your heart and mind for anything that hinders you hearing Him. If anything comes to

---

3   Adapted from Joy Dawson's principles of intercession found in her book *Intercession*.
Dawson, Joy. *Intercession: Thrilling and Fulfilling*. Seattle, Washington: YWAM Publishing, 1997.

mind, confess and deal with it so nothing stands between you and Him.[4]

3. Admit your knowledge is limited at best, and you need His Spirit to guide you as you pray. Set aside any agenda you have and recognize He knows better than you about what's on His mind and in His will. Lay aside your own thoughts and imagination and ask Him to help you to hear only His Spirit without your own ideas interfering.

4. Deal with the Enemy. Satan likes nothing more than to distort the communication between you and God — and any others with whom you're praying. Take the authority Jesus has given us over Satan and tell him to get lost and take any of his demons with him.

5. Thank God, in faith, for what He will speak. Expect Him to speak to you clearly.

6. Wait and see what He says. Some common ways He speaks are through passages in the Bible, bringing to mind phrases or songs, or showing you a mental picture. (I've listed other ways He has spoken later in the chapter.) Remember: don't be discouraged if you don't hear anything right away. This is a process that takes time.

7. If you're praying in a group, take time for each person to share what God spoke to him or her. Many times, people may have heard something that makes no sense to them, but when shared in a group, it is the vital piece that brings understanding to the whole message God wants to speak.

---

4   It is important to note the difference between conviction and condemnation. If God brings conviction, it is done in love, and will not bring feelings of shame or condemnation. If you feel shame, worthlessness, or condemnation in relation to what comes to mind, that is not of God. Tell Satan to get lost and take his accusations with him.

8.   Once you have heard Him (and shared among the group), repeat back to Him what you heard and ask if there is more He wants to share. He may bring more clarity to things you don't fully understand.

9.   Take any action steps God is asking of you or the group. Pray through the things you are hearing.

10.   Finally, leave the burden of what you've heard with God. Many times in intercession, God will ask you to partner with Him in prayer for the huge things on His heart. Continue to pray for those things as He leads you, but know you are not meant to carry the weight of the world with you. If God has asked you to carry a burden, He will give you the grace to carry it, but the major weight is His to bear.

I am sure other great lists of steps to hearing God are available. I love that God doesn't fit neatly into a box we carry with us. The above process worked for me as I was learning to hear Him; however, if it doesn't work for you, ask God to reveal Himself and the ways that He speaks to you. Be open to new things each time you pray because He will not always relate to you in the same way. He is the Creator of the universe, and that creativity is evident in the ways He chooses to speak.

> Be open to new things each time you pray because He will not always relate to you in the same way. He is the Creator of the universe, and that creativity is evident in the ways He chooses to speak.

Whatever process you use, look forward with anticipation to what He will speak to you because it is always exciting to see what God will say. After all, He is the Master of the universe, and He wants to converse with you. That in itself is pretty incredible! Not to mention that when He speaks, planets can be conjured and light created! Imagine what can happen in your life when His words create new realities in your world.

Following is a short list of some of the ways he has spoken to people throughout the ages.

1.   Angelic visitation – Mary (Luke 1)

2.   Personal visitation – Saul/Paul (Acts 9)

3.   Audible voice – Samuel (1 Samuel 3)

4.   Handwriting on the wall – Belshazzar/Daniel (Daniel 5)

5.   Vision – John (Revelation)

6.   Dreams – Joseph (Genesis 37)

7.   Nature – Jonah (Jonah 1),

8.   Signs and wonders – The plagues in Egypt (Exodus 7–11)

9.   Prophets – Isaiah, Jeremiah, Ezekiel, etc.

10. Counsel of others – Nathan/David (2 Samuel 12)

11. Burning foliage – Moses (Exodus 3)

12. A donkey – Balaam (Numbers 22)

13. Stories – The Parables of Jesus

14. God's Word – The Old Testament quoted in the New Testament (Luke 4)

I love how out of the box God is! If He can speak through a donkey or a plant, He really can use us! One other thing I love is knowing He is the same — now and forever — as He was in the stories listed above. The list is just a small sampling of the ways He has spoken, and He is still showing Himself faithful to speak to us today.

One of my favorite stories of hearing God in my own life came about as I was praying about a move to Ireland. I'd been praying and feeling for weeks that I needed to go there. Then one day, I got word that the school I hoped to work with wasn't happening. I was devastated because I felt so certain I needed to be in Ireland, that God had something for me there.

As I cried and asked God how this could be, when I'd been so sure I heard Him, I walked into the bathroom of the cabin where I was staying at the time. On the shelf sat 7 boxes of Irish Spring soap. A whisper in my spirit told me I would have an Irish spring. Six days later, I was invited to move to Ireland for a year. Six months after that invitation, I was living there — just in time for spring!

I have many more stories of hearing God, but some of my friends have allowed me the privilege of sharing their stories of hearing God's voice as well. So I'll share those testimonies with you.

1) *"While we were preparing to go to the Philippines on our outreach with a missions school, our passports were returned with our visa stamps. All of us students were excited to see the 'welcome' stamped our passports. What surprised my family was that most other students had received a single entry visa good for 90 days. Though we applied as a class, some received different types of visas. My family received a multiple entry visa good for 5 years. Was God 'saying' something to us?*

"On our first evening in the Philippines, I was moved by and concerned with the conditions there. As we were walking back to our hotel we could see the pollution in the headlights of the oncoming cars. It was an eerie experience for me and I said, 'The Lord would have to speak very clearly for me to bring my family back here again'. Well, I guess that's not a problem for Him. During our outreach there we fell in love with the people. In the next 5 years we went back to live there for about 7 months and made several more trips to bring other schools and meet with our dear friends. We still think of the Philippines often and pray that the Lord will 'speak' to us again and send us back there." – K.F.

2) *"Many years ago when I was a teen, I felt the Lord telling me that someday I would be on the mission field. Actually, it was more than that... Jesus placed a burning desire and a dream to take his Love and Hope to a country beyond my own. With that thought in mind, I picked a college major that would be beneficial, did a missions trip after high school, etc. However, the opportunity just didn't present itself after college. The years went by and many times I revisited this dream to serve the Lord abroad, but each time I felt it just wasn't quite the right time yet. At any time, I could have forced it to happen, but ultimately I wanted what He thought was best for me so I waited...and waited...and...*

"Now, after 20 years, things seem to be starting to move this direction — oddly enough, just when I had finally resigned myself to the fact that maybe I had misunderstood Jesus all those years ago. Like Joseph in the Old Testament, He needed to prepare me for the work ahead before launching me into it. I had a lot of emotional baggage in my early 20's and though He can use us no matter our imperfections, I needed to let Him heal me before I could help others find His healing. And I have learned some valuable skills through work and ministry over the years that will serve me well in any culture." – L.W.

3) *"My husband and I had left the church we were pastoring and were waiting on God for His next steps of direction for us. We knew that He was leading us into missions but needed His confirmation. While my husband was out of town for a week, we agreed to both wait on God for words of direction. When he returned we would share what God showed us. We found out later, after comparing stories that God spoke to each of us the same day, giving us the same scriptures. The words from God were from Isaiah 61:1–7. We have seen God fulfill His Word to us, as we have been serving in missions now for more than 21 years. God is faithful to His Word & His promises."* – P.F.

4) *"I was 23, pregnant and alone. When I told the father that I was pregnant he told me to 'take care of it' and cut me out of his life. I made an appointment for an abortion.*

"Nauseous and shaking in the doctors' office, I was suddenly overcome with a sense of calm. Everything around me was a blur except for two words on the medical release in front of me: GO and HOME. I closed my eyes and silently asked 'was that for me? Am I supposed to go home?' and as clear as a bell I heard: 'YES, E.'

"I went home and started researching adoption agencies. Six months later I gave birth to a little girl. Eighteen years later we became friends. Thank God." – E.W.

I love listening to and reading stories of our Intimately Infinite God! Throughout this book, I will continue to share stories of hearing God's voice in various ways. We'll also dig further into the wonders of communication with the Creator of the universe in the next few chapters as we look at increasingly intimate stages of relationship we can share with Him.

QUESTIONS TO PONDER:

1. Is the idea of hearing God's voice new to you?

_____

_____

_____

_____

_____

_____

_____

_____

2. In which ways has God spoken to you?

_____

_____

_____

_____

_____

_____

_____

_____

_____

RECOMMENDED ACTIVITIES:

1. Study verses about the Shepherd, for example, Genesis 48:15–16, Psalm 23, Isaiah 40:11, 64:8, Matthew 9:36, John 10, Hebrews 13:20–21, 1 Peter 2:25, 5:4, and Revelation 7:17.

_____

_____

_____

_____

_____

_____

_____

2. Set aside a block of time when you can be quiet with God and wait to hear what He will say. Write down what you hear.

_____

_____

_____

_____

_____

_____

_____

_____

_____

CHAPTER FOUR

FRIENDS OF THE MASTER

"The beauty of grace is that God already knows about our sin. He just wants us to be honest with Him." – Derwin Gray, *Limitless Life*

So we've discussed hearing God talk to us, but what about talking to Him? That's easy! It's called prayer, and we start praying the minute we recognize our Creator and ask Him to save us from our selfishness. Then as we learn His voice and rest in His care, we move into relationship with our Shepherd. As His sheep, it is easy to stay focused on our own needs and the provision and protection He offers.

Master & Servant

As we continue to listen to His voice and become more focused on what we can offer Him, we move into the Master/servant stage on the relationship continuum. When in this stage, we can refer to several passages in the Gospels where Jesus tells stories involving masters and slaves to illustrate our service to Him. We are indeed servants of the Master, and He does ask us to do things for Him. As with the parable of the talents (Matthew 25:14–30), our Master has given us talents and treasures to steward. We are responsible for what we do with everything our Master has given us, and as servants, we are accountable to our Master.

The problem many followers of Christ have at this stage is they live their entire Christian existence stuck here. We become slaves to the task and not to the Master. We are tied down by rules and regulations, instead of released in the freedom to be in relationship. Unfortunately, this often leads to forgetting the Shepherd, the One who carries us and cares for us. We begin to do tasks out of routine, obligation, or even fear because we have forgotten Who the Master is; He is Love. He is our Gracious King.

> We become slaves to the task and not to the Master. We are tied down by rules and regulations, instead of released in the freedom to be in relationship.

A pendulum within the Church swings, almost violently, between the grace of God and the fear of the Lord. On one side, we have churchgoers who quote Proverbs 9:10, saying the "fear of the Lord is the beginning of wisdom." They are not wrong. Too often, however, this fear is mistaken for the terror of a God who is just waiting for us to fail, so He can send lightning from heaven to remind us who is boss.

When taken to extremes, this side of the swinging pendulum sends us into hiding from our Master lest He decide He's had enough of us. The rules and regulations we try to live under become a weight we can no longer withstand, so we crumble. Some spend their lives still struggling under the weight in hopes they can measure up. Others cast off the weight completely and decide that since they can't measure up, there is no point in trying. Some go so far as to say there is no God, no absolute truth, and no limits at all.

On the other side, we have churchgoers who see the danger of turning the fear of the Lord into this horrible, terrifying weight. In response, they declare that God's grace is the only thing on which we should focus. No matter what you do, God will still love you regardless. They are not wrong either. But too often, this grace is mistaken for a license to live however we choose.

When the pendulum swings too far in this direction, we end up saying, "all roads lead to heaven; believe whatever you want and live however you want because a loving God will never send anyone to Hell." Not only are rules tossed out the window, but the good news of God's saving grace is no longer relevant or necessary.

> Yes, our Master is full of mercy and grace. And yes, our Master is awesome and powerful. He has the ability to hurl a lightning bolt at us if He chooses, but He doesn't.

Both of these extremes are damaging to the Church and to our witness in the world. Yes, our Master is full of mercy and grace. And yes, our Master is awesome and powerful. He has the ability to hurl a lightning bolt at us if He chooses, but He doesn't. He is to be feared, but not in the way so many misunderstand. He doesn't want us to live in terror, but in awe and reverence and wonder of His greatness and majesty. He truly is an incredible God, and when we see how vast and awesome He is, then His love, mercy, and grace for us become that much more significant.

Once we understand the way He cares for us despite His greatness, it becomes a bit easier to wrap our thinking around the fact He wants to be more than our Master: He wants to be our friend. In John 15:15, Jesus says, "No longer do I call you slaves, for the slave does not know what his master is doing; but I have called you friends, for all things I have heard from my Father, I have made known to you." God wants us to move to a deeper level of intimacy with Him as His friends, which leads us into the next stage of relationship with God.

Friends

The definition[5] of friend is "one attached to another by affection or esteem" or "a favored companion." That is what Jesus calls us! Now, I've never been a slave, but I've been an employee. In my experience, communication is a lot different between an employer and employee than among friends. Typically, friends share more deeply about life. It is two-way communication on a more intimate level.

Communicating with God

When I think of intimate, two-way conversations with God, I reflect on King David. If ever there was a person who was honest with God, it would be him. Take a look at Psalm 13:

How long, O LORD? Will You forget me forever? How long will You hide Your face from me? How long shall I take counsel in my soul, having sorrow in my heart all the day? How long will my enemy be exalted over me? Consider and answer me, O LORD my God; Enlighten my eyes, or I will sleep the sleep of death, And my enemy will say, "I have overcome him," And my adversaries will rejoice when I am shaken. But I have trusted in Your lovingkindness; My heart shall rejoice in Your salvation. I will sing to the LORD, Because He has dealt bountifully with me.

I love how honest King David is when he is talking to God. My favorite line of the worship song "Unashamed Love[6]" says, "You are worthy… Of a childlike faith, and of my honest praise, and of my unashamed love." Honest praise. Psalm 13 is honest praise. In the midst of everything David went through and all the thoughts of despair, he still praised God. He recognized the faithfulness of His God and praised Him, right after despairing of life. You may think this sounds a bit unbalanced or even bipolar, but I think it is honest praise.

---

5   "Friend." *Merriam-Webster.com*. Merriam-Webster, n.d. Web. 19 Jan. 2016.

6   "Unashamed Love" by Lamont Hiebert. Album: Ten Shekel Shirt: *Much* ©Integrity/Epic (2001).

I spent much of my life pretending to praise God in the midst of my circumstances. I can't speak for anyone else, but I believe many people in the Church today pretend well. During the time I was seventeen and feeling invisible, it was because I chose not to be seen. I was a professional pretender. I praised God in word and song while inside, I considered stepping into the path of a bus. I was fighting the urge to "sleep the sleep of death," and no one knew the difference. My praise was not honest if it was even praise at all. I thought it was genuine praise at the time, but looking back, it was all part of an act.

I wonder how many people in the Church could win Academy Awards for the performances they give each week. Many of these church performers are living in the Master/servant stage as I did for so many years, but they have forgotten Who the Master really is. Some may be like the Pharisees — whitewashed tombs, looking great outwardly, but inside they are dead. They exist in a lifeless religion of endless rules, and they have lost the relationship with the Master. Too many live in fear of telling the Master and their peers where they really are spiritually and emotionally. They may lose their job, their position among believers, and maybe even their salvation and place in heaven.

I believe this breaks the heart of God. He wants us to trust Him to the point where we share with Him the deepest desires and sorrows and joys of our heart. Often we try to hide our heart from Him because of fear or shame, but we forget He already knows our thoughts and feelings. He can see the fathomless depths of our being, and He loves us anyway!

He is also so great that he can handle anything we might say. We cannot surprise God. He has already seen and heard it all, and He knows better than we what is inside us. So why not tell Him? Why not be honest and truly communicate with Him—not just prayer consisting of a list of needs and wants but real gut-level, honest communication? He loves it, and He will respond — not by pounding us into the dust from which we are made, but by proving He is worthy of the trust we place in Him when we give Him access to the deepest places of our heart. He will not force us to open up, but I can tell you the words He speaks in that place of vulnerability can heal wounds and bring light to darkness like nothing else can. Time does not heal wounds; being in His presence through honest and open communication with Him does.

Anyone who knows me well knows I am a talker. I am a verbal processor. I must process thoughts out from my head and into words before I clearly know what I am thinking. I previously required a person to sit and listen to me in order to think. During my time overseas, I learned to process my thoughts and feelings into written words. God provided a friend to be my sounding board via email. More importantly, I learned to process with God through journaling.

In the years since then, my journal has become my lifeline. I am convinced if anyone ever read my journals, I could be locked up because of some entries. I have some writings that sound nuts, and many others that are simply not true. I have written down lies the enemy has planted in my mind through some of the events in my story. Those lies creep into my journal before I'm even aware of their existence. As I'm writing, I can often identify the flaws in my thinking and the lies of the enemy. I usually write them on a different piece of paper, which I then burn. I use this technique to offer those lies to the All Consuming Fire Who is able to burn them out of my heart and mind. Once I have rid my mind of such junk, it is time to listen to truth from the One who brings healing and peace to my heart.

> As I'm writing, I can often identify the flaws in my thinking and the lies of the enemy. I usually write them on a different piece of paper, which I then burn.

But what of those times when I don't hear a response? Is God ignoring me? Does He take a break? Am I doing something wrong? Have I offended Him to the point that He gave up and walked off? My heart hurts, and I think He's nowhere to be found. Those times are truly a struggle to walk through, but I'm beginning to realize those are also the times that bring me to new places with Him.

The Silent Valleys

I'm learning that without walking through the valleys with God, the mountain tops mean very little. I have experienced times on top of the mountain and heard God clearly. It was easy to believe everything He was speaking because I could feel it. I *knew* He was there, that He loved me, and that I was on top of the world with Him. And then came the valley.

I have become aware I rarely walk slowly down a nice little path into valleys. One minute I'm walking along the mountain top with God, then suddenly, I'm tumbling quickly downhill sustaining bumps and bruises along the way. When this happens, I often think I left God at the top of the mountain shaking His head and wondering how I missed my step. Or I think perhaps He is walking on with the 7 billion plus other people He has to worry about, not realizing I have disappeared from His presence. It sounds ridiculous to even write this, but it's what my feelings have told me is happening. It feels as though His voice comes from miles away if it even comes at all.

> I have become aware I rarely walk slowly down a nice little path into valleys. One minute I'm walking along the mountain top with God, then suddenly, I'm tumbling quickly downhill sustaining bumps and bruises along the way.

What I have learned during my recent trips through valleys is these feelings are simply not true. He is not shaking His head in disappointment or ignoring me. The truth is He descends into the valley with me, and walks with me always. At times He is silent, but always for my good. Without the times of questioning, searching, and struggling through the darkness, I begin to take His presence for granted. It is in those times I realize my need for Him, and I begin to seek Him above all else once again. When He is silent, I become desperate for Him to come and speak; nothing else matters. I feel I have lost much ground in my relationship with Him, but in reality, I am drawing closer.

When the silence is broken, I realize I have reached a more intimate place with Him.

The deeper the valley we walk through, the higher the mountain top is on the other side. The key is to seek Him and talk to Him even in those times when it seems your words go no higher than your room's ceiling. Pray as King David did. Remember God's goodness, and praise Him for it. Be honest with God about where you are. Scream and cry if you need to. God can handle it, and He will respond. It may happen at the last possible moment, but when you think the "sleep of death" is your only pleasing option, He will meet you in that place of brokenness. He will come and He will speak and He will heal your heart. He is the Friend who is closer than a brother!

QUESTIONS TO PONDER:

1. Do you feel the freedom to be completely yourself with God? With others?

_____

_____

_____

_____

_____

_____

2. Have you experienced the silence of God and then the deeper intimacy on the other side as a result?

_____

_____

_____

_____

_____

3. Do you spend your time with God reciting a list of needs and wants and reading a certain number of verses, or do you actually communicate with Him?

_____

_____

_____

_____

_____

_____

RECOMMENDED LISTENING:

1. "The Silence of God" from the album *Love and Thunder* by Andrew Peterson

   _____

   _____

2. "Mountain of God" from the album *Wherever You Are* by Third Day

   _____

   _____

3. "Stained Glass Masquerade" from the album *Lifesong* by Casting Crowns

   _____

   _____

RECOMMENDED READING:

4. The Psalms of David

   _____

   _____

RECOMMENDED ACTIVITIES:

5. Write your own psalm to God.

   _____

   _____

   _____

   _____

   _____

   _____

CHAPTER FIVE

OUR PARENT, WHO ART IN HEAVEN...

"A parent's love is whole no matter how many times divided."
– Robert Brault

God, our Father

When I was a kid, if I got hurt and needed someone to kiss my "booboo," I ran to Mom. When I wanted to buy something, I went to Mom. But when I wanted to do something a little adventurous, I asked Dad first. You see, it was unthinkable in our home to ask the second parent for anything if you had already been turned down by the first. As most kids do, I learned quickly which parent to ask for what I wanted.

I mention this to illustrate how in many cases each parent fulfills a different role. Mothers are the more nurturing. Fathers challenge us to go further. For instance, my dad threw me into the deep end of a pool to teach me to swim. He knew I could do it; I simply needed the nudge to overcome my fear and get into the water. Often, mothers are the caretakers and fathers are the providers. So why is it important to discus the roles of mothers and fathers? Because both male and female are created in God's image, and He fills all roles. He is the nurturer, provider, encourager, challenger, healer and so much more. He knows how to meet us wherever we are.

I love the images manifested in the book *The Shack* [7]. The main character, Mack, is invited for a weekend with God. When he arrives at the shack, he is greeted by Papa, a "large beaming African-American woman" who smells like Mack's mother's perfume. Mack has never had a good relationship with his father, and God knows he would not accept Him as Father. The female version of Papa was there to nurture and bring healing.

Later in the story, a time of reconciliation takes place with Mack and his father. Then, the following day, comes a time when Mack has to overcome very difficult circumstances and is challenged to forgive in the face of immense pain. That morning, Papa comes in the form of a father — an older, dignified man with a gray ponytail. He is there

---

7   *The Shack* by William P. Young
     Young, William P. *The Shack*. California: Windblown Media, 2011.
     In this book, a man is struggling with grief and anger in the wake of his daughter's disappearance and murder. He receives an invitation from "Papa," the name his wife uses for God. The invitation is for a weekend away at the cabin where his daughter was killed.
     When he arrives, he finds that he is spending the weekend with all three members of the Trinity - "Papa," Jesus and the Holy Spirit. Throughout the weekend, he is confronted with his belief about God, himself, suffering, grace, forgiveness and more.
     The book is not meant to be a theology book, and there are aspects of it I wouldn't hold as truth. However, I love some of the pictures portrayed of God's interaction within the Trinity and with His children. If you choose to read it, "eat the meat and spit out the bones." Take in what is helpful and let the rest go.

as a source of strength and encouragement to Mack to overcome and be more than he thinks he can be.

God comes to us in a form we can understand and approach. Of course, He does not become something He is not in order to make us comfortable, but neither can we put Him in a box. He is so much more than we can imagine. To limit our encounters with Him by our puny imagination is to do Him and ourselves a huge disservice. He is our Father and wants to draw us into a special place of intimacy with Him as His children.

I know many people who have difficulty accepting or even understanding this level of intimacy with God. I know of two main struggles with accepting God as a Father. The less obvious is to imagine God as a Father who is better than the father of our earthly experience. This was my struggle, and I was unaware of it until just a few years ago. I have a wonderful relationship with my parents. I grew up as daddy's girl, and I cannot imagine having a better or more loving earthly father than I already have. In my mind, I thought my dad was as good as it gets, and even God couldn't outdo him. My dad would tell me, obviously, that it was a lie.

The more apparent struggle is about those who have not had a good experience with their earthly father. I know many people who have struggled to imagine a good relationship with a "Father." A good friend of mine turned her back on God at the age of eight because of this bad relational dynamic. She was taught early and throughout life that God is our Father, and based on who her male role models in life were, she wanted no part of it. I am heartbroken when I think of how many people have struggled or continue to struggle with this issue.

Satan has attacked the family concept so viciously and with such ferocity that I believe he wants to damage our idea of God as Father. I also believe understanding and accepting this facet of our relationship with God is key in moving to the final stage of intimacy and in finding our identity and purpose. So much is meant to come through our relationship with our earthly parents (e.g., identity, values, inheritance, on so on) that I believe it is the same with God the

Father. He wants to extend His legacy through us, His children, and Satan is desperate to stop it.

When I read about the patriarchs in the Bible giving their blessing to their offspring, I think how amazing that is. Look at what Isaac said when he blessed Jacob: "Now may God give you of the dew of heaven, and of the fatness of the earth, and an abundance of grain and new wine; may peoples serve you, and nations bow down to you; be master of your brothers, and may your mother's sons bow down to you. Cursed be those who curse you, and blessed be those who bless you" (Genesis 27:28–29).

When Esau discovered Jacob had lied to their father and had stolen his blessing, he "lifted his voice and wept" (Genesis 27:38). He begged his father for a blessing of his own. This was a big deal.

Most of Genesis chapters 48–49 are about Jacob blessing his own children and grandchildren before he dies. He named each of his sons and Joseph's sons and spoke destiny over them. Genesis 49:1 states, "Then Jacob summoned his sons and said, 'Assemble yourselves that I may tell you what will befall you in the days to come.'" Some blessings were great; others not so great. But he spoke destiny and blessing over each of his children: "He blessed them, every one with the blessing appropriate to him" (v. 28).

> How sad that many fathers (and mothers) don't give their blessing to their children today.

How sad that many fathers (and mothers) don't give their blessing to their children today. I know that in the major life decisions I make, I crave the blessing of my parents — not to mention God's! And God longs to give us His blessing as we seek to move into His purposes for our lives.

Read over the blessings from the patriarchs of the Old Testament in Genesis 27, 48–49. These fathers were inspired by God to speak over their children. Their words hold truth and identity and destiny. It is wonderful when earthly fathers make the effort to see what God is saying about their children and affirm those messages in them. But consider hearing it directly from the Source!

When Jesus was baptized and released into His ministry, God blessed Him. The Spirit of God came in the form of a dove and a voice spoke, "This is my Beloved Son, in whom I am well pleased" (Matthew 3:17). God is speaking that and much more over us! He is the One Who knit us together and makes us who we are. He knows what and who we are, better than any person on earth. When He speaks blessing over us, it is an incredible experience. He speaks of our original design.[8] I know people who have been given a new name by their heavenly Father that reflects their purpose and destiny. And unlike Isaac, God is not limited to blessing only one child with the dew of heaven. He is free to rain down the blessings of heaven on all His children!

> God is not limited to blessing only one child with the dew of heaven. He is free to rain down the blessings of heaven on all His children!

At one time, I struggled with feeling I was completely alone and unnoticed. I wanted to have someone's undivided attention. I heard a whisper in my heart saying I had my Heavenly Father's undivided attention. Instead of feeling comfort, I felt anger. How could He give me undivided attention when He had seven billion other children to watch over?

Later that night a friend came to my door with a piece of paper. She had been praying for me and had felt God had given her a word for me. She had written down that I was a princess, and that God loved

---

8   God created each of us with a unique design, a design that enables us to live and reign with Him forever. Satan's forces and our own selfishness have inhibited our ability to see and live out our original design; however, God will restore it as we grow in intimacy with Him and surrender our will to His. When we reach heaven, selfishness and sin will be no more, and we will be completely restored to the Creator's original design for us.

me. She encouraged me to read Psalm 139. As I did, verse 6 struck me: "Such knowledge is too wonderful for me; it is too high, I cannot attain to it." I realized then I didn't have to understand how God is great enough to give several billion people His undivided attention. I couldn't understand; my brain would explode. I simply had to trust it was true. That same Father is ready to pick you up, set you on His lap, and give you His undivided attention.

So, what does it mean to be a child of God? He wants to bless us and speak destiny over us. Great! How do we move past the idea that God cannot be better than our experience of fathers, whether good or bad, here on earth?

The first step is to realize this assumption is a lie. No matter how good or bad your earthly father was or is, God is infinitely good! He will never abuse you in any way. He will never take his anger out on you or on someone close to you. He will never berate you or make you feel worthless. He will never break a promise or forget a special day.

Yes, He cares so much about each aspect of your life that He knows your birthday and everything else. He counts the hairs on your head, for goodness sake. I can't say I've received a card in the mail postmarked heaven, but I have seen the most gorgeous sunset over a river and known it was painted especially for me in that moment as a gift from my Abba. And yet, as much as He delights in giving good gifts to His children, He won't spoil us either.

A scary notion for many is the idea of God the Disciplinarian. Many have experienced a parent or some other authority figure who has used "discipline" in the form of abuse; if not physical abuse, then emotional, verbal, or even spiritual abuse. As with the Master, the idea of being disciplined by a Father who can see everything we have ever done can be terrifying if we have the wrong idea of His character.

Actually, it is the loving nature of God that requires Him to discipline us. Proverbs 13:24 states, "He who withholds his rod hates his son, but he who loves him disciplines him diligently." Discipline is never fun, but it's what the loving Parent does. He does not get so angry that He lashes out in frustration, but He always confronts our sin in love. He is love; He can be nothing else.

I also know people, and have at times been one myself, who are afraid to come forward in prayer in a group setting when God is moving and blessing others. Something holds us back from asking for our own blessing — or, at least, from asking for it publicly. The fear is God will embarrass us in front of the group — as though He is a cosmic hypnotist Who will make us cluck like a chicken in front of everyone or maybe let us fall to the ground — and what if no one is there to catch us?

God is not out to publicly humiliate anyone. He knows each person intimately and knows what we can handle. He will not belittle you with a blessing or with discipline. He will bring humility and a right understanding of who you are and where you need to grow, but will never disgrace or shame. If you feel humiliation and condemnation in the midst of correction, it is not of God. You are listening to the wrong voice.

Were you ever made to feel like you were lovable only when you were obedient? I must admit that on many occasions, I have found it difficult to love people who are not behaving to my liking. It is an excellent thing I'm not God. His love is unconditional, and nothing you can do will ever make Him love you more — or less!

That doesn't mean we should do whatever we want without regard to His commands or His Word. It simply means we don't obey out of fear but love. While thinking on this subject one day, I realized my view on obedience had changed. God will not ever love me more or less than he does right now. No matter what I do, that won't change. What changes is whether His love for me brings Him joy or pain. Think about that for a moment. Within our choices, we hold the power to bring joy or pain to the heart of God!

Our heavenly Father will also never make you feel worthless. You have value simply because you are His. He paid the ultimate price to purchase you out of slavery and to bring you into His family as a son or daughter. Not only are you a child of God, but also you are His favorite. There is not, nor has there ever been, nor will there ever be a person on this planet whom He loves more than you! He loves you, and that gives you more worth and value than any precious stone or metal or any other thing in creation. That is the image your Heavenly Father has of you, and He longs for you to walk in the knowledge of your worth.

If you struggle with letting God be your Father, it may be helpful to practice calling Him "Father" in some way. Abba, Daddy, Papa, Father, whatever is comfortable for you. Instead of always addressing Him as God or Lord, address Him in the intimate terms of the family relationship. This is one way to recognize Him in that role. It may be very difficult at first, but training your heart to talk to Him as a Father is a good start.

> Not only are you a child of God, but also you are His favorite. There is not, nor has there ever been, nor will there ever be a person on this planet whom He loves more than you!

As you begin to think of Him in that way, He can redeem any experience you've had of earthly fathers to show you what it means to truly be fathered. Ask Him to reveal Himself to you in ways that will show you what it means to have Him as a Father. He wants to challenge you, to discipline you when necessary, to love you, to comfort you, to provide for you, to teach you, to nurture you, to bless you, to give you a legacy and an inheritance of nations, and so much more. Come to Him as a child and see what He will do!

As God reveals Himself as a Father, it frees us to accept His view of us. When we see ourselves as our Father sees us, it helps us to accept how loved we are — not only by our heavenly Father, but also by the Lover of our soul. We are the Beloved!

QUESTIONS TO PONDER:

1. What is your relationship with your earthly parents like?

_____

_____

_____

_____

_____

2. Do you have a difficult time relating to God as a Father?

_____

_____

_____

_____

_____

3. Does the idea of God as a parent scare you? What frightens you about it?

_____

_____

_____

_____

_____

4. Do you need to forgive your parents for anything in order to feel the freedom to be a child of God?

_____

_____

_____

_____

5. Have you ever experienced something you knew was a gift from God that was intended just for you?

_____

_____

_____

_____

_____

RECOMMENDED READING:

1. *The Shack* by William P. Young — Read the story and glean what God shows you of Himself.

_____

_____

RECOMMENDED ACTIVITIES:

2. Take some time to talk to God as your Father. Ask Him what blessing(s) He speaks over you, and write down the answer(s).

_____

_____

_____

_____

_____

_____

_____

_____

_____

_____

CHAPTER SIX

THE BELOVED

"I am my Beloved's, and His desire is for me." – Song of Solomon 7:10

I went to a Rich Mullins concert in the mid 1990s. He was a remarkable musician and a funny guy. I remember him telling a story about his grandmother giving him a Bible when he was young. According to his story, she had torn Song of Solomon out of the Bible and told him he could have that particular book of the Bible when he got married. He ended the story by saying that at 40 years of age, he had yet to read it.

I laughed along with everyone else, but the truth is, I know people today who have never read Song of Solomon because it is only for those who are married. I wasn't interested in reading it myself for much of my life until I was introduced to a study by Mike Bickle called *Song of the Bride*. It totally changed my perspective on this book of the Bible because it helped me to see the principles of intimacy with Jesus as His Beloved Bride.

Because of the amount of information Mr. Bickle gives in his twenty hours of teaching on the eight chapters of Song of Solomon, it is impossible for me to capture it all in this book, let alone in one chapter. However, I'd like to share with you just a few insightful points into our relationship as the Bride of Christ.

The Song is the story of the growth of a Bride into a woman who will follow her Lover into the dangerous places of life and service. Most interesting to me are the two times she searches for him. In chapter two, the Lover comes and asks her to go with Him, and she refuses out of fear. But then she begins to feel the lack of His presence. He hides his face from her, and in the beginning of chapter three, she is searching everywhere for Him. His absence called her out of her comfort zone. Finally, she finds Him and holds on for dear life.

At the end of chapter four, she experiences a change of focus. Through His words, spoken to her and over her, along with the experience of growing in intimacy with her Lover, she matures to the point of focusing her concern selflessly on Him. Just as she arrives at this point, she encounters another trial. The Lover comes and calls to her again, and this time she responds in obedience, only to find His presence has been taken away again. Not in discipline this time, but in testing.

The leaders, or watchmen, in the city mistreat her as she searches for Him. It is as though the Lover is asking if she will continue to follow Him even when she cannot feel His presence and in the midst of negative circumstances, and especially since the promised Divine blessings are not delivered in the way or timing she expects. Her answer is a resounding yes! She continues to seek Him and follow after Him. She even teaches others to seek Him until she is in His presence again.

Also interesting to me is the meaning of "your eyes are like doves" (1:15c). Doves are significant for several reasons. First, they are among several species of birds that mate for life. Second, they are often used as a symbol of love. Last and even more significant is that unlike many species of birds whose eyes work independently of each other, doves have binocular vision — their eyes work in unison to focus on only one thing at a time. Whatever they are looking at gets their full attention and focus. When Jesus is our Lover, He says our eyes are like a dove's, and He is celebrating the fact that our gaze is on Him alone. No matter what else is going on around us, our eyes are fixed only on what we see through and in Him.

I also love the first phrase of chapter one verse five, "I am dark but lovely" (NKJV), because of the intended contrast. She recognizes the darkness (or sin) she has been marked by, and yet she is able to affirm her loveliness. It reminds me of the scene in the story of Isaiah in which the prophet recognizes he is "a man of unclean lips" and accepts the cleansing of the hot coal touching his lips (Isaiah 6:5–7).

We are dark. We are stained by the sinful nature we are born into. But we must also realize we are lovely. We have been cleansed and must accept the truth that our Lover is captured and enthralled by the loveliness He sees in us. Beauty really is in the eye of the Beholder.

Many other aspects of the study impacted me, but I will share just one more. Song of Solomon 6:5 (NKJV) states, "Turn your eyes away from me, for they have overcome me." He praises the fact she has eyes only for Him, so obviously, He is not asking her to turn her eyes away. He is simply saying her eyes of devotion have conquered Him. Give that a minute to sink deep into your heart. We have the power to overcome the heart of God. He cannot be overwhelmed or conquered by all the forces of hell or by any force on earth, but His heart is conquered by the loving gaze of His Beloved.

Have you ever been in love? Ever experience the longing for the one you love to choose you and love you in return and felt the elation when he or she did? Ever feel the ache of emptiness that seems only that one person on earth can fill? Ever wait with anticipation for a phone call, email, or text from the object of your affection? Ever feel your heart decide whether to stop or speed up when you hear his or her voice after a long absence — or even a short one?

If you have felt or can imagine feeling any of these emotions, then you have seen an infinitely small glimpse of how God feels about you! He waits with anticipation for every time you will say His name. He longs for you to choose Him. He waits with anticipation to spend time with you and hear what's on your mind and heart. He is the Lover of your soul and every other part of you.

One day, several years ago, as I was lamenting my singleness, I asked God what was wrong with me. Why in my mid-twenties had no guy really ever given me a second look, (except maybe that one guy when I was 14)? The still, small voice in my mind and heart whispered to me God had not given me a second glance either because from the moment He caught the first glimpse, He couldn't tear His eyes away!

That is how God feels about me, and it's how He feels about you. If you have given your heart to Jesus, then you are His Bride. He is wild about you! If you have not yet surrendered to His love, this is still how He feels about you. He is captivated by you, and He longs for you to choose Him today and every day forever.

> If you have given your heart to Jesus, then you are His Bride. He is wild about you! If you have not yet surrendered to His love, this is still how He feels about you.

That last statement may sound odd, but it's true. Every minute of every day we are bombarded with things that take our attention. We choose every day and even every moment on what our focus will be. The One who is madly in love with you longs for you to choose Him today, even if you have been in a relationship with Him for decades. He craves time with you alone.

In the last several years, I have started going on "dates" with Jesus. Sometimes, I will take my journals to a park or coffee shop. I buy a croissant, a coffee, or a dessert and find a comfortable chair by a fireplace or the water, and I spend hours just being with Jesus. Sometimes, I write in my journal and process. Sometimes, I just sit in His presence in the peace of the beautiful surroundings, and sometimes I fall asleep. The point is I set aside a block of time to be with Him.

Obviously, this idea doesn't work for everyone. Maybe you would prefer to go running with Jesus. The important thing is to make time for Him in your life and even let Him romance you. Choose to bring Him along in whatever your day holds, and set aside time to focus on Him. Yes, He is omnipresent and, therefore, already wherever you're going, but how often are you aware of His presence there? Acknowledge Him and make Him a part of your life every day and not just when you visit the church building.

Can you imagine a relationship between lovers who only see and talk to each other once a week? It sounds ludicrous to most of us. Who would choose that kind of relationship with their loved one? And yet, that is how so many live with regard to the Lover of their souls. Some people have locked God into a cell in the local sanctuary and visit Him in that small prison for an hour or two each week. They go one day a week to an obligatory meeting, and that is their only connection point to God.

The human heart longs for adventure, romance, and beauty. The only place we can find the true versions of any of these things is in God.

He longs for so much more, and so does your heart. If you truly listen to the desires of your heart, you will hear it is crying out for Him. The human heart longs for adventure, romance, and beauty. The only place we can find the true versions of any of these things is in God. He invites us into the adventure of walking through life and ministering with Him each step of the way. He desires to romance us and show us His love in ways big and small. And He wants to show us His beauty in the world and in us and, in turn, empower us to share His beauty and love with others.

QUESTIONS TO PONDER:

1. Is the idea of God as Lover new to you?

_____

_____

_____

_____

_____

2. Have you ever experienced being God's Beloved? How did it feel?

_____

_____

_____

_____

_____

3. How often do you spend time with Jesus, not out of duty, but just to be with Him?

_____

_____

_____

_____

_____

4. What would your ideal date with Jesus be? A movie? A walk in a park? Take out and a sunset?

_____

_____

_____

_____

RECOMMENDED LISTENING:

1. *The Song of the Bride* teaching series by Mike Bickle[9]

_____

_____

RECOMMENDED READING:

2. *The Sacred Romance* by John Eldrege and Brent Curtis

_____

_____

RECOMMENDED VIEWING:

3. In preparation for the next chapter, I highly recommend watching the *Lord of the Rings* trilogy — extended editions if possible. Better yet, read the books!

_____

_____

RECOMMENDED ACTIVITIES:

4. Get away with God, just the two of you for at least an hour. (Maybe go on your ideal date from your answer to question 4 in the previous set of questions.) I would go so far as to say if you've not done this before, leave your Bible at home. Think out of the box on what time with Him looks like.

_____

_____

_____

_____

_____

---

9   Audio recordings, transcripts, and study notes are available at www. mikebickle.org/resources/series/song-of-songs

QUESTIONS TO PONDER FROM PART 1: INTIMACY

1. Of the levels of relationship with God, which ones do you identify with? What others have you experienced that aren't discussed in this book?

_____

_____

_____

_____

_____

2. Have any of these chapters changed your view of your own relationship with God? In what ways?

_____

_____

_____

_____

_____

_____

3. How does an awareness of the stages of intimacy with God influence the way you relate to Him?

_____

_____

_____

_____

_____

_____

_____

Part II: Identity

"He made you — on purpose. You are the only you — ever. Becoming ourselves means we are actively cooperating with God's intention for our lives, not fighting him or ourselves." – Stasi Eldredge, *Becoming Myself: Embracing God's Dream of You*

CHAPTER SEVEN

SHIELD-MAIDEN OF HEAVEN

"You are a daughter of kings, a shield-maiden of Rohan..." – J.R.R. Tolkien, *The Two Towers*

During the first several years of my full-time missions work, I continued to struggle with who I was meant to be. I identified some of my struggles were related to trying to be my brother instead of myself, but I wasn't sure what to do about that. Obviously, I needed to be myself, but I had no idea who that was. I moved to Central Asia for a couple of years and learned much about God, the world, and people, but very little about myself.

I spent eighteen months of my two years in Central Asia in Afghanistan. During that time, I was given opportunities to use my nursing skills by being a part of a community health education project. Several days a week, I met with three of our staff, who were Christians.

We read the Bible, prayed together, and I taught them basic health lessons. They would then teach those lessons to people in the Uzbek and Turkmen[10] villages near our town. I originally thought it would be great to use my nursing training, but I later realized I hated it. I enjoyed the opportunity to meet, pray, and read the Bible with Afghan believers. But the health education aspect of my role and learning the Uzbek and Turkmen languages was very stressful.

After nine months, I was allowed to begin overseeing the literacy project — visiting classes where women and girls were taught to read and write, paying teachers' salaries, writing simple books for students to practice reading, and doing administrative work for the project. This change also meant I could begin learning to speak, read, and write Dari — a language I enjoyed. I felt much more fulfilled in this next part of my time there because I connected with what I was doing — helping women and girls learn to read. Working with the literacy project had nothing to do with the medical training I had received, but I knew it was what I was supposed to be doing while I was there.

> I originally thought it would be great to use my nursing training, but I later realized I hated it. I enjoyed the opportunity to meet, pray, and read the Bible with Afghan believers.

In those nine months, I was pushed toward a role that needed to be filled because my skills fit the requirements. Others saw me as Stephanie Hall, RN, but in reality, that was not who I was. It had been my signature at times, but it certainly didn't fit who I felt I should be. My skills don't make up who I am. A nursing license is a small representation of the skills I have learned, but that is not a full picture of Stephanie Hall. I learned through my

---

10   There are at least a dozen ethnic groups in Afghanistan and as many languages. The region of Northern Afghanistan where I lived is largely populated by Uzbek and Turkmen people. In the nearby villages, these (Turkish based) languages are the primary languages spoken, though the common national language in the region is Dari (Persian).

experiences in Afghanistan that too often we look at pieces of paper or outward appearances and judge who a person is.

During the time I was living in Central Asia, I read *Captivating* by John and Stasi Eldredge and worked through the accompanying journal. I answered every journal question in the order presented. If I needed to think more in-depth about a specific question, I stopped reading until I could answer it fully. Most questions gave me no problem until I got to the one that asked, "If you could be any character from any story, who would you choose and why?"

That question took me a week to answer because I thought through every story I could remember. I truly wanted to choose the right character. I'm not sure why it was so important to me, but I spent hours thinking about that simple question before I settled on my choice — Éowyn of Rohan from *Lord of the Rings* by J.R.R. Tolkien. With that question finally answered in my mind, I went on with my reading and mostly forgot about it for nearly a year.

A few months after I returned from Afghanistan, I had prayer time with a dear friend, and God began to give me glimpses of who I was created to be. Together, we asked God to show me who I really was in His eyes. I heard God say I was a "shield maiden of heaven." My friend saw a picture of a woman in battle. As we shared with each other, I realized God was giving us pictures and descriptions of Éowyn, the character I had chosen nearly a year earlier.

Lord of the Rings was already one of my favorite stories, and it has become more special to me over the years. Each time I read the story or watch the movie, I become aware of new things I can learn from Éowyn's story. Throughout the next couple of chapters, I want to share some of this story and how it has helped me shape my own understanding of who I am.

We'll start with some background information on Éowyn for those not familiar with her story. Éowyn is the niece of the King of Rohan. She was raised as his daughter since both her parents died when she was very young. She has an older brother named Éomer, who is a great warrior. She has spent several years caring for her aging uncle and father figure, King Theoden, who has fallen under an enemy's spell. She is stalked by the king's "advisor," Grima Wormtongue, who has received the promise of her hand in exchange for his service to the enemy in bewitching the king. Her life seems pretty bleak.

She longs to do something epic and valiant with her life, but she is a woman in a world dominated by men. As the men she knows and looks up to ride off to defend the people and land they love, she is left behind to tend the kingdom. Although she is left in charge, in a place of leadership and responsibility, she wants to be riding off to fight alongside the men.

One particular scene always impacts me. In it, Éowyn is practicing with a sword when a man, Aragorn, approaches and comments on her skill with the blade. She responds: "People without swords can still die upon them. I fear neither death nor pain." He asks, "What do you fear?" Her response always hits close to home. "A cage. To be kept behind bars until use and old age accept them, and all thoughts of valor have gone beyond recall or desire."

I believe she sees femininity and her identity as a woman as the cage that will keep her locked up and insignificant. I know the feeling. That was the basis of my younger years as a "feminist." I hated being held back and did everything I could to prove I didn't deserve the distinction of being a girl, that I could be let out of the cage to fight with the men.

All the while, just like Wormtongue, the enemy of my soul was there whispering I would always be alone, telling me my tears would always go unnoticed by others, and he alone was aware of my anguish. Not only that, but he was also skilled in tempting me with options to bury my loneliness and turmoil in thoughts and activities that would bring temporary relief. Fortunately, I never developed an interest in drugs, alcohol, or sex. Perhaps he knew I wouldn't do those things, but thinking couldn't be a sin, right? I'm sorry to say I gave in and spent far too many hours escaping into my mind's own fantasy world, daydreaming scenes in which I could find significance.

Aragorn's response to her fear of a cage makes my heart skip a beat because it speaks so deeply to my heart. "You are a daughter of kings, a shield maiden of Rohan. I do not think that will be your fate." When he said that line, something or Someone whispered to my heart, "You are a daughter of the King, a shield maiden of heaven, and that will not be your fate." It spoke of a freedom to be significant, even as a woman. It promised a release from my self-imposed imprisonment and the chance to do big things for God.

•••

Before I share more of what I've learned from Éowyn's story, allow me to address the gentlemen readers for a moment. Men, don't get bored and check out because this doesn't apply to you. Women are not the only ones to be attacked in this way. It breaks my heart to see how the Enemy has attacked men and broken down the masculinity of men in my generation and those younger.

I'm not talking about guys getting mani/pedis, and I know manly men are out there. However, as a former "feminist," I want to apologize to men for the convincingly told message that we don't need you. I believe a huge victory was won for the Enemy when women rose up and took on the role that men should have in society. I believe that's also part of the reason for the breakdown in families.

> However, as a former "feminist," I want to apologize to men for the convincingly told message that we don't need you.

Now, do I believe all women should be married and "barefoot and pregnant in the kitchen?" *No!* If I believed that, I would have no self-respect because I am currently neither of those things. But I think in the push for "equality," women stole something valuable from men — the identity God gave them as strong warriors, providers, and protectors. In the process, women were also robbed of the freedom to need men in those roles.

Even within the Church, the attributes most often praised lean more toward the nurturing, compassionate, patient, sensitive side. When I read about Jesus, I do see Him as compassionate and patient in His teaching of the disciples. I also see Him driving out money changers from the temple with a whip, challenging His followers to grow in what some may consider harsh ways, and correcting those He loves with firmness. Yes, some men have become violent and abusive, and that is wrong. But, sometimes, it seems modern Christianity teaches men that to be Christ-like, they have to be feminine.

> When I read about Jesus, I do see Him as compassionate and patient in His teaching of the disciples. I also see Him driving out money changers from the temple with a whip, challenging His followers to grow in what some may consider harsh ways, and correcting those He loves with firmness.

I understand I'm generalizing and stating strongly an issue that is not universal. I am simply making the point that we (women, Christianity, and civilization as a whole) need men to be men — warriors who will fight for what's right, who will rise up and lead their households, who will protect those who need protection, and who will pursue and fight for the ones they love. We need to see the attributes of God that are unique to men represented in the Body of Christ. Men, please rise up and take your place as warriors and leaders in the Kingdom of God. We desperately need you to be the men He created you to be!

•••

Now, back to our story where we rejoin our heroine at my favorite part of the movie. Éowyn has gone against the wishes of her uncle, disguised herself as a man, and ridden to battle with the men. (Yes, I see a bit of myself in even her rebellion, but I pray the rebel in me has been redeemed.) Her uncle has been mortally wounded and is about to be devoured by a great beast ridden and controlled by the Witch King. Both the beast and its master are fearsome creatures not to be trifled with.

When Éowyn sees the beast advancing toward her uncle, King Theoden, she steps in between them and announces that she will kill the beast if it dare touch her king. The Witch King urges the beast forward and Éowyn, true to her word, chops off the beast's head.

Now she has to face the Witch King. Because "no living man" can kill him, his boldness betrays him. Éowyn is not alone in the battle at this point; she is aided by a hobbit — Merry,[11] who stabs the Witch King in the back of the knee, bringing him to his knees. Éowyn pulls off her helmet, lets her hair down, and announces, "I am no man!" She thrusts her sword into the Witch King's face and defeats him; however, she is severely injured. But he is no more. He shrivels into a pile of dust and is carried away by the wind.

Although I have seen this movie many times, that part never fails to make my heart leap with excitement. The first few times I saw it, it was simply the excitement of the victory that made my blood rush a little bit faster through my veins. Now as I see myself in the story and look for what God wants to teach me, I get excited because her victory speaks to me. The very thing Éowyn sees as her greatest weakness is the one thing that makes her victorious!

---

11 Hobbits are a race known for staying to themselves and avoiding adventures. Yet these stories include four of them who changed the fate of Middle Earth - Frodo, Sam, Pippin and Merry.
They were also known to be very small. Merry was known in history as the tallest, and yet reached just barely above 4 feet. Because of his size, he was told by the King of Rohan to stay behind as the army rode to battle.
Éowyn allowed him to ride into battle with her to join his friends on the battlefield.
How many times do we discount what someone else has to offer because we don't see what's inside. Éowyn knew how it felt to be left behind, and she made sure her friend was not left behind again. In the end, her choice likely saved her own life, and the dignity of her uncle and King, Theoden.

Satan is a created being; therefore, he doesn't know all that God does. He doesn't know the future any more than we do; however, I do think he perceives more than we do. I believe he sees our strengths and potential long before we do, and in my experience and observation, he attacks those things very early on.

In Éowyn's case, the Witch King does not perceive the threat of her gender or try to keep her from coming to battle. Her life and the ideas of others do a good job of that without his help. I believe that can also be the case with us. Life and the ideas and words of other people can do a great job of planting lies in our minds or obstacles to fulfilling our destiny. However, in addition to life and the impact of the words of others, I also believe we have the added factor of an enemy, who though limited in his knowledge, knows more than we realize.

I may be wrong about his perception of our specific strengths, but he has been around a very long time and has seen a lot of people. If nothing else, he has seen God and knows His power and creativity certainly more than I do. I believe he starts very quickly to look for our strengths and to begin to break them down before we ever perceive them. Long before I could see the good of my femininity, I had swallowed the lie it was a weakness and not to be embraced or used for God's glory.

This issue is not just about gender either. Mine is simply the lie I swallowed for many years. It can be any strength God has given you that is attacked. We were all created for a purpose and designed with that purpose in mind. The easiest way for the Enemy to keep us from fulfilling that purpose is to attack our identity and make us believe we are not valuable or able to do the very things God has created us to do. If we are constantly comparing ourselves to others and trying to be someone other than who He made us, we cannot do what we were made for simply because it keeps the focus on us and not Him. For the record, you can't do what God has purposed for you unless you do it in His strength. That keeps the focus on Him, us in relationship with Him, and ensures all the glory is His!

One day as I was walking around Kunming, China, I felt God ask me to pray for a friend who was struggling. I began to pray, and suddenly a voice in my head said I had no right to fight on his behalf. The voice then said my friend didn't want my prayers. If he didn't want to fight this spiritual battle himself, it was pointless for me to try. For the entire walk, I fought this voice by declaring I had every right to pray and fight for him because God had given me authority by asking me to pray for him. I said my friend was struggling and didn't have the strength to fight for himself, so God was raising up others to fight for him.

When I arrived back at the hotel and began writing in my journal, I asked God what all that was about. I didn't accomplish anything in prayer time because I spent the whole time defending my authority to pray for him. Then, in my mind, there was Éowyn taking off her helmet and declaring, "I am no man." I realized she could have killed the Witch King without telling him of her authority to do so, but the declaration and acceptance of her identity gave her the courage to do it. My time of walking and declaring my authority to pray on behalf of a friend was my own realization of my authority to follow God's direction.

> For the record, you can't do what God has purposed for you unless you do it in His strength. That keeps the focus on Him, us in relationship with Him, and ensures all the glory is His!

This situation taught me a valuable lesson about declaring truth. It may not change anything in the battle itself, but it has a great impact on the person who chooses to stand on the truth.

One other realization I had during this conversation with God is that some of my greatest victories come when I am fighting on behalf of others. Éowyn wanted to win renown and be known as a great warrior, and she achieved that with her victory over the Witch King. However, at the time she stepped between the beast and King Theoden, her concern was not her own fame but the life and dignity of her uncle and king. She won the very thing she hoped for by laying it aside and protecting her loved one. God has made it clear to me that my strength comes in loving others and fighting for them instead of fighting for my own desires. I venture to say your greatest victories will come in that way, too. God loves to honor those who humble themselves and put others ahead of their own ambitions.

One final observation I want to point out in this scene is that Éowyn was not victorious over the Witch King on her own; she was aided by Merry. We are not meant to do life alone. God Himself said it was not good for man to be alone. God in the Trinity has been in relationship for eternity. He is a relational God, and that is a major part of His image that He placed in us. We need one another!

The most profound impact of Éowyn's story on my life I have yet to reveal. I discuss it in the next chapter.

QUESTIONS TO PONDER:

1. What in your life represents the "cage" that holds you back?

_____

_____

_____

_____

_____

_____

2. What do you consider to be your greatest weapon?

_____

_____

_____

_____

_____

_____

3. What has been the greatest victory in your life so far?

_____

_____

_____

_____

_____

_____

RECOMMENDED ACTIVITIES:

1. Because the previous chapter had many recommended readings and viewings, you get a break on this chapter unless, of course, you want to tackle the reading of the *Lord of the Rings* trilogy.

CHAPTER EIGHT

TRUE LOVE CONQUERS ALL

"Then the heart of Éowyn changed, or else at last she understood it. And suddenly her winter passed, and the sun shone on her." – J.R.R. Tolkien, *The Return of the King*

In this chapter we delve into my favorite part of Éowyn's story. Although I summarize, I still recommend you read the trilogy. What I discuss here is from *The Return of the King* in the chapter titled "The Steward and the King." Éowyn is in the Houses of Healing recovering physically from her encounter with the Witch King, but her spirit is still lost in the shadows. Her hopes of dying valiantly in battle have been dashed. Her brother and Aragorn, the man she believes she loves, have gone with all the other warriors to another great battle where death is almost certain. Once again, she is held captive this time by the Warden of the Houses and the orders of Aragorn, the King of Gondor.

When she voices her discontent to the Warden, he takes her to the Steward of the city who is also a patient in the House of Healing. The Steward, Faramir, will not change the Warden's mind about Éowyn going into battle with the others. He invites her to walk freely in the garden and to spend time with him. He says,

"It would ease my care, if you would speak to me, or walk at whiles with me… if while the sun yet shines, I could see you still. For you and I have both passed under the wings of the Shadow, and the same hand drew us back."

"Alas, not me, my lord! Shadow lies on me still. Look not to me for healing! I am a shield maiden and my hand is ungentle."

Her reply isn't exactly encouraging, but she does spend time with him in the days that follow. They begin getting to know each other. Then, one day, word comes to the city of the final victory over the evil that has threatened all of Middle Earth. The battle is won! Evil is gone for good, and everyone is celebrating. Everyone except Éowyn, that is. She is invited by her brother to come and join the returning heroes, but she refuses to go celebrate with them. Faramir, who has been released from the Houses of Healing, is summoned by the Warden to talk to Éowyn.

"Alas, not me, my lord! Shadow lies on me still. Look not to me for healing! I am a shield maiden and my hand is ungentle."

When he inquires as to why she will not go, he can think of only two reasons she might stay back. The first is she is upset the invitation came only from her brother — and not Aragorn. The second is she wants to stay close to Faramir. Or perhaps the answer is both, and even she cannot discern the primary reason. He finishes his questioning by asking, "Éowyn, do you not love me, or will you not?"

Éowyn responds that she wanted someone else to love her, but she doesn't want anyone's pity.

Faramir's response is a bit long, but I love to read it. It makes my hopeful romantic heart flutter. He tells her he knows she wanted Aragorn to love her because of her admiration for him and his position and the renown she would gain. When she received only pity from the king, however, she decided a brave death in battle was the next best thing. He tells her she is a valiant lady who has won renown of her own. He also declares she is more beautiful than even the Elves could put into words. He finishes his speech by saying that at first he felt pity because of her sorrow, but now even if she had all of her heart's desires and became the Queen of Gondor, he would still love her.

> "'I stand in Minas Anor, the Tower of the Sun,' she said, 'and behold! the Shadow has departed! I will be a shield maiden no longer, nor vie with the great Riders, nor take joy only in the songs of slaying. I will be a healer, and love all things that grow and are not barren.' ..."

"Then the heart of Éowyn changed, or else at last she understood it. And suddenly her winter passed, and the sun shone on her.

"'I stand in Minas Anor, the Tower of the Sun,' she said, 'and behold! the Shadow has departed! I will be a shield maiden no longer, nor vie with the great Riders, nor take joy only in the songs of slaying. I will be a healer, and love all things that grow and are not barren.' And again she looked at Faramir. 'No longer do I desire to be a queen,' she said.

"Then Faramir laughed merrily. 'That is well,' he said, 'for I am not a king. Yet I will wed with the White Lady of Rohan, if it be her will.'

"... And to the Warden of the houses Faramir said, 'Here is the Lady Éowyn of Rohan, and now she is healed.'"

With one declaration of love, Faramir brought her out of the Shadow and freed her heart! That is the most important lesson I've learned from Éowyn's story: The only thing required to be fully healed and fully free is a revelation that we are loved.

I love the statement that maybe she just finally understood her heart. We have desires in our hearts we may never recognize until they arrive in our life, and we then realize they are what we have longed for all along. Éowyn thought she wanted the love of Aragorn because of what he represented in her mind. She "loved" him only for what she would get from him — honor and glory. When she couldn't be Gondor's queen, the next best option, as she saw it, was a valiant death in battle. Not until she experienced true love, offered with no expectation of anything in return, could she know what she was longing for.

When she finally understood her heart's desire, she also realized who she wanted to be. I love how she transitions from saying, "don't look to me for healing because I'm a warrior," to, "I'm not going to fight anymore and compete with the warriors, but I will be a healer and love all that grows." She now knows who she really is. Realizing she is loved immediately silences that voice in her mind that has kept telling her all her life she must be like her brother or others in order to be accepted.

In a society that honored and revered the Riders of the Mark or warriors and protectors of their homes, and growing up surrounded by her brother and other men and boys destined for the honor and glory of that position, her hope of honor and acceptance must have seemed to lie only in battle. Despite the fact she was loved and respected by the people of Rohan, she believed the lies she was alone and unloved until Faramir spoke the truth, and it reached into her heart and freed her to be who she truly was.

What I find most fascinating about this moment is her choosing to become what she had been fighting against all along. She had always been asked to care for others — protect and lead her people to safety, care for her sick uncle — yet she scorned that role and wished to die rather than be left out of the action. Then, in the moment her heart learned she was loved, she chose to be what others had always known her to be, who she truly was at heart — "a healer and lover of all things that grow and are not barren."

So many times I have done this same thing. I listened to the father of lies tell me I was alone and unloved, so I looked for my chance to gain the love of someone through various actions. And when I didn't think that was working, I looked for a way to die a brave death even if only in my imagination.

It has been a long process for me to accept the truth I am loved by God and others. Since I began to learn about myself through the story of Éowyn, I have learned much about being a strong woman of God who is willing to fight for those I love. Until I discovered this part of her story, however, I was missing the most important lesson she had to teach me. When I read the trilogy and discovered this lesson, I wanted to experience the freedom Éowyn found in Faramir's love — the freedom to be fully myself.

It wasn't until a very difficult trip to Europe in 2009 that I had the revelation I needed in order to feel that freedom. I was on staff then with a missions training course, and through a series of circumstances, I ended up leading an outreach team by myself. Along with my team of two guys and two girls, I spent 10 weeks traveling through Amsterdam, four cities in Germany, Prague, and finally London. We served and shared with people where we could, praying, and continuing to learn about God. It was a good time of growth for me, but also a huge struggle to walk in the truth of what God had said about me instead of the lies that constantly bombarded my mind and heart — lies that told me I was worthless and not a good leader.

One morning, about three weeks before the trip was over, I sat in Nürnberg, Germany, lamenting I was a failure as a team leader. I had believed the lies of the enemy, and I was quite sure that each member of my team believed them to be truth as well. I was questioning God's wisdom and plan, telling Him how wrong He'd been to trust me with these people, and doubting my worth as a person in general. As I sat there praying, it suddenly dawned on me. I was agreeing with the wrong voice.

God had recently told me during a prayer time with my team that I was His Beloved, and yet here I was agreeing with His Enemy instead. When that realization came, I chose to stand on the truth of God's words instead of what my head was telling me. I stood against the lies of failure, worthlessness, and hopelessness and chose to believe God knows more than I do, that I could trust His assessment of me more than my own.

Once I made that choice, the rest of the trip was different for me. I still had moments of uncertainty and some huge difficulties awaiting me during those last three weeks. Circumstances were very much the same as they had been, but I was different. God had spoken to my heart the declaration that set me free to know my true identity as His Beloved, and just as importantly, I had chosen to believe it.

> Understanding you are the Beloved of God is life changing. Nothing else can free us to be ourselves in the same way. Truly knowing and feeling we are chosen — despite having nothing to offer in return but our own choice to be His — is something words cannot describe.

Understanding you are the Beloved of God is life changing. Nothing else can free us to be ourselves in the same way. Truly knowing and feeling we are chosen — despite having nothing to offer in return but our own choice to be His — is something words cannot describe. I hope each one of you experiences the freedom found in this level of intimacy with your Creator — the freedom to walk confidently in your identity.

QUESTIONS TO PONDER:

1. Have you ever "loved" someone only to realize later it was the idea of the person or what he or she had to offer that you truly loved?

    _____

    _____

    _____

    _____

    _____

    _____

2. Have you ever wished for a "valiant death" or sacrifice in order to gain honor or attention?

    _____

    _____

    _____

    _____

    _____

    _____

3. Have you ever experienced a love that frees you from all expectation and allows you just to be you?

    _____

    _____

    _____

    _____

    _____

    _____

CHAPTER NINE

LIES & STORIES

"If you continue in My word, then you are truly My disciples; and you will know the truth, and the truth will make you free." – John 8:31–32

You now know a large part of my story and how I have discovered my true self. I share more of my journey in the chapters to come as we talk about discovering God's intentions when He knit us together. But before we move on, I want to underscore that my story is not the important one in this book. It is simply a tool I use to share what I've learned. This book is really about your story and, hopefully, helping you to make sense of it.

I mentioned in the first chapter how Satan is desperate to keep us from progressing in our relationship with God or realizing our potential. His attacks are often focused on our greatest strengths and even our deepest dreams, and some of the greatest weapons in his arsenal are lies. He is the Father of lies, and while there are millions and billions of specific lies, it is amazing to me how many boil down to the same common roots.

As you may have noticed in the first part of my story, I struggle with lies that tell me I'm insignificant or "less than." At one time, the lies told me I was less significant because of my gender. More recently, they tell me my story is less interesting than someone else's and no one will care to read what I write. The message is still that I am not significant enough to do what I know I'm called to do, but it sounds different than what it used to.

We have looked into my story, and I want to spend just a bit of time allowing others to share their stories, too. Insignificance is only one of the lies in the Enemy's arsenal. Maybe you identify with that struggle, or maybe you don't. I have been given the privilege to share the following stories to give you perspectives from others about the lies they have battled in their own lives. As you read them, allow God to speak to you about the weapons the Father of Lies has used in your life.

1) I literally didn't even feel human. I felt like a ghost floating through the lives of others. That's how bad my insecurity was.

I graduated college in three years. Took first place in state in archery, third place in nationals in karate. My work has been recognized by state agencies and trade groups.....and I am the least accomplished of my family.

My mother was beautiful and warm and everyone loved her. My father was a powerful military officer. My grandfather, a war hero. My aunt, a brilliant artist. My brother was the golden child of the family: amazingly charismatic, strong character, smart-but-not-bookish. Captain of the football team who married the head cheerleader and never got in trouble. He was everyone's favorite, even mine.

I am cross eyed and off beat. Very friendly but not good with people. Very intense and nerdy. Bullied in school from about 1st grade. A hard teenager to raise. Always fighting that "Not enough, you aren't doing enough, are not enough. Too much and not enough".

I thought if I could just do a little more…. I truly thought "If I could win the Nobel Prize (that was my 'little more'!), then, THEN people would have to acknowledge my worth. I would be….enough".

But honestly, I would still be thirsty, dying, parched. The problem was not my accomplishments. It was not how pretty or ugly I was. It was not how fabulous my brother was, or even how mean other people were.

Somewhere along the way, I decided that God felt the same way about me that I and others did: I was not enough. That I had to earn His love. That I was Esau to my brother's Jacob. Always in trouble or always about to be in trouble.

The Holy Spirit helped me realize that I was calling God a liar. I was CALLING GOD A LIAR! I was reading His Word, the very breath of Jesus and calling it a LIE!

I understood the words "Holy and dearly loved", but I didn't "feel" them. I let the enemy's lies of me not being enough permeate through my heart and spirit and mind. I kept saying "Yeah, but" every time I started to dare hope in the love of God ("Yeah but I am not as good as my brother. Yeah but other Christians don't always like me, so what is wrong with me? Yeah but I know my inner sinful nature.").

That is how one real lie of the enemy alters reality to make us live in a lie — he sets up lies like a false gravity in our hearts and we bounce against walls and furniture unless we refuse to move from our Anchor, until we believe the truth.

So when the enemy tries to make me think I am not enough, I am not lovable, I simply go back to "Steph, don't call God a liar". If God says that I am DEARLY loved, then I am

DEARLY loved, whether I feel it or not, whether other people see it or not, whether I think I should be or not.

The Lord's love for those who are saved is infinite and expansive and not dependent on us, but on Him. It is HIS character, not mine, that I needed to rely on. It is about HIS goodness. It is about how much His Son's blood is worth.

I am enough because His Son was enough. And that is enough. – S.D.R.

2) A lie lived in my heart — quiet, unseen. I ignored. I pretended it didn't exist. But it did.

I loved God. I sought Him. I followed Him. I wanted to be used by Him. But I didn't believe Him.

Sure, I knew in my head that God is good. He wants to bring healing to the broken places; He wants to liberate us from the snares of this world and show us a brand-new, unimaginable life. I believed every bit of it was possible… for everyone else. I didn't believe it for myself.

At one point, I was glaringly confronted with the lie lurking inside me. I had been waiting on God for what seemed like ages to answer a prayer — a deep cry — of my heart, and He seemed to do nothing but delay. I don't know why, but this time God opened my eyes to see that I didn't believe He would be good to me. I believed that He would withhold the good thing I greatly desired. Something inside me broke. I cried out to God because I knew I could not fix myself.

I prayed on my own and with fellow believers. And as was planned at that time in my life, I went on a mission trip to West Africa. I prayed that God would heal me during the trip. And so He did — wonderful, giving, and GOOD God that He is.

He spoke softly to my heart and mended me in many ways, but the most impactful involved luggage. I travelled with eleven people. I was still hurting from the knowledge that I didn't believe God would be good to me, and the first thing to happen when we arrived was that my luggage was lost. The only bag to be lost. Figures, right?

Things can sometimes be lost a long time or forever (particularly in parts of Africa). I remember sitting by myself, trying not to freak out, trying to make sense of it. I could only think about the fact that I had no underwear but what I was wearing, I had one extra pair of clothes in my carry-on, I had no shoes but those on my feet, and the things I had brought for celebrating Christmas (it was late December) were all in my bag.

As I sat quietly, praying, hoping I wouldn't break down in tears, I sensed God speak to my heart. He said, "You have two options here. You can freak out — that's an option. Or you can let me be your Father and provide for you."

I sat stunned, and then said out loud, "You are my Father. I trust you. Please provide for me."

I kid you not — by the end of the night, I had a bag with clothes contributed from the other girls on my team; I had a pair of lightly used sandals; and crazily enough, the missionary had a pack of brand-new, unused underwear that were my size. I had everything I needed.

It was beautiful, and the beginning of my heart's healing. To top it off, I continued to pray about my lost bag, really wanting to be able to share what I'd brought to make Christmas special. At 10pm on Christmas Eve, 13 hours away from the airport I'd flown into a week earlier, I heard my name being called. I left my room in answer to the call, only to hear, "Your bag is here! They found your bag!"

God is good to every single one of His children, and I will not believe anything else. – C. K.

QUESTIONS TO PONDER:

1. What lies have you believed about yourself?

_____

_____

_____

_____

_____

_____

_____

2. Do you see a pattern or a shared common root in those lies?

_____

_____

_____

_____

_____

_____

_____

3. How have lies held you back? What have you not done because of them?

_____

_____

_____

_____

_____

_____

_____

RECOMMENDED ACTIVITIES:

1. Write out the lies you've believed about yourself on a piece of paper, then dispose of it somehow. (I prefer fire.) Then journal your thoughts.

_____

_____

_____

_____

_____

_____

_____

2. Don't neglect to spend time allowing God to fill your heart and mind with truth! Ask for specifics and Scriptures. Write down the truth that He speaks; read it often, memorize it and believe it!

_____

_____

_____

_____

_____

_____

_____

_____

_____

CHAPTER TEN

FREEDOM OR RUBBLE

"… when a king forgets who he is, he looks for himself in the rubble of conquered cities. He is haunted by a bottomless pit in his soul, and he will pour the blood of nations into it until the pit swallows the man himself." – Andrew Peterson, *North! Or Be Eaten*

I love this opening quote. The first time I read *North! Or Be Eaten*, I paused at these sentences and read them several times. These words screamed about the importance of identity to me. When people forget who they are, their first instinct is to begin conquering something and finding worth in the victory. Perhaps you don't conquer cities; maybe it's the fight for a promotion at work, striving to get accolades for one achievement or another. We seek to build ourselves up in some way to gain the value we are missing because of our lost identity. We are haunted by the subsequent emptiness, and whether it is "the blood of nations" we pour into it, or simply careless words that tear down someone else while elevating our own ego, we leave casualties behind in our aftermath.

Amazing things happen when we have new and deeper revelations of our relationship to God and the identity we have in Him. No matter which stage of intimacy you find yourself at today, God can show you something amazing about who you are to Him. Whether or not you have yet to receive the revelation of yourself as His friend or child or beloved, you can still see yourself in His light and know a bit more about who He has created you to be.

As amazing as the results of revelations of our identity are, the consequences that can result from losing sight of our identity are just as powerful. For me, it is entirely too easy to lose sight of who I am, and I begin to look for "cities" to conquer. I find friends with faults and much like the Pharisee's prayer, I think "at least I don't do that." I have built my beautiful façade of an identity on the wreckage of the identities of those I love, whom I have destroyed in my fight to feel better about myself.

Amazing things happen when we have new and deeper revelations of our relationship to God and the identity we have in Him.

The previous paragraph illustrates clearly where the problem lies. Read through those few sentences again, and notice how many times in those few lines the words "I," "me," and "my" appear. We begin to lose sight of who we are as soon as we lose sight of Whose we are. The moment my focus shifts from God to myself, I have lost myself. I can only be the person He created me to be when I keep my focus anchored on the unchanging One in the relationship — God.

To illustrate how our search for identity can harm those around us, we must go back to the story of when I was leading the team in Europe at a point before I began to walk in the truth. I had firmly fixed my eyes on me, what I was doing well, where I was dropping the ball as a leader, and mostly how much I felt I had failed at leading.

A member of my team was struggling, and in trying to make myself feel better, I determined I would help. Oblivious to my motives — and the terrible outcomes prideful motives nearly always cause — I ended up looking for my identity amongst the rubble of my relationship with this person. Of course, I found little more than hurt for both of us, causing a strained relationship with someone I was meant to lead for another month.

Fast forward to that morning in Nurnberg, Germany, when I chose to stand on God's truth about me as His beloved rather than accepting the Enemy's lies. Unfortunately, that determination did not fix my past mistakes. The friendship with my teammate was still in ruins, and I had to deal with the consequences of my well-meaning but backfiring words. The difference was now I knew who I was in the process. My heart still broke for the hurt I had caused, and I still longed for the relationship to be restored, but my identity was no longer tied to the acceptance of this person. As much as I cared for this person and his well-being, I was released to be me without his stamp of approval, and it changed the last three weeks of the trip for me.

> Oblivious to my motives — and the terrible outcomes prideful motives nearly always cause — I ended up looking for my identity amongst the rubble of my relationship with this person. Of course, I found little more than hurt for both of us.

Those three weeks were not easy. Words pierced my heart on several occasions, and I shed many tears in secret (and some in the open). Through it all, though, I was able to give love in the best way I knew how, even when it felt like none of it was accepted or returned. I had an unlimited source of love pouring into me because I knew I was loved by the King of the universe. He was my only focus and even if no person on earth ever gave me love, I wouldn't lose His affection. I knew my identity as the Beloved of God, and with my eyes on Him, I was free to love others no matter what!

The only thing to be found in the rubble of conquered cities and individuals is just that: rubble and ruins. The only place to find out who you are is in Him. You are created in His image, so looking at Him is the only way to see what you are meant to be.

So, why do I keep harping on this issue of identity? Yes, it's important to me, but it's more than that. I believe it's one of the most important concepts we must all grasp. It has implications for every part of our lives, and I believe it is one of the greatest issues facing my generation and the ones to follow — perhaps even the generations before mine! I understand that more now than ever.

I'm sure you've figured out in the course of this book I want to be married. I have moped about my singleness every few months (sometimes more often) for more than a decade now. Looking back, though, I am so thankful God did not allow me to marry someone at 20 or 21 like I wished I had. I had no clue who I was or wanted to be back then. Now, I know not only who I am (more than ever before), but also what direction I want to go with my life. This knowledge will make all the difference in recognizing the man I can travel with through this life when the time comes.

Maybe you are someone who got married young, and it has worked for you. Or perhaps it didn't work. Whatever the case, the impact on a marriage is only one example of the possible implications of knowing your identity in Christ. And knowing our identity is only half the journey. We must put into practice the revelation of who we are in Christ.

For each of us that journey will look differently, and I cannot give you a map to show you the route. The road is different for each person, but the direction we're all heading in is the same. We are moving farther along the road to finding and walking in the purpose for which God has created us!

QUESTIONS TO PONDER:

1. What have been the implications in your life in learning your
    true identity?

    _____

    _____

    _____

    _____

    _____

    _____

    _____

    _____

    _____

    _____

2. Have you ever stood in the ruins of someone you love because of
    your words or actions?

    _____

    _____

    _____

    _____

    _____

    _____

    _____

    _____

    _____

    _____

3. Have you ever felt so full of God's love that you could pour it into others and build them up no matter the response you received?

_____

_____

_____

_____

_____

_____

_____

_____

_____

_____

RECOMMENDED LISTENING:

1. "Loose Change" by Andrew Peterson

_____

_____

RECOMMENDED READING:

2. *The Wingfeather Saga* by Andrew Peterson — includes *On the Edge of the Dark Sea of Darkness, North! or Be Eaten, The Monster in the Hollows,* and *The Warden and the Wolf King* — This is a series of fantasy books for young adults that I love, and the themes of identity and purpose are interwoven throughout all four books.

_____

_____

Part III: Intention

"God's purpose in saving you was not simply to rescue you and keep you busy until He shipped you off to Heaven. His purpose was much bigger; he commissioned you to demonstrate the will of God 'on earth as it is in heaven,' helping to transform this planet into a place that is radiant and saturated with His power and presence." – Bill Johnson, *Spiritual Java*

CHAPTER ELEVEN

DELIGHT YOURSELF

"I will be a healer, and love all things that grow." – J.R.R. Tolkien, *The Return of the King*

For what purpose were you created? This is a huge question — a question that takes years for most of us to answer, and many people never decide on an answer. From the time we can speak, we start telling adults what we want to be when we grow up. Most of us change our answer a hundred times before we're teenagers, and then we really get fickle. I have heard that up to 80% of college students change their major at least once, and the average college student changes majors three times.

Purpose is not just the occupation on which you settle either. So much more is involved to being fully the person you were created to be than choosing the "right" career. Knowing your purpose will determine how you spend your time, talents, and treasure. It affects every area of life because identity and purpose are at the core of our being. When we are walking in the truth of who we are and why we were created, we can experience a level of fulfillment that many only dream of feeling.

I often think of the moment when Éowyn finally knew who she truly was. She was then free to walk in that knowledge. "I will be a healer, and love all that grows." That's quite a change of tune from her previous mantras. Yes, obviously the change affected her career choice, but it was more about who she wanted to be, and it would affect how she responded in every aspect of her life.

It's like that with us as well. For some of us, the knowledge comes quickly and revolutionizes our lives. For others, it is a long process that may take years to realize. Many facets comprise our make-up, with different ways to live out each one. None of us will "arrive" at the fullness of this journey on this side of heaven. New things to learn and deeper levels of freedom to experience will always be available to us throughout our lives. "For now we see in a mirror dimly, but then face to face; now I know in part, but then I will know fully just as I also have been fully known" (1 Corinthians 13:12).

> None of us will "arrive" at the fullness of this journey on this side of heaven. New things to learn and deeper levels of freedom to experience will always be available to us throughout our lives.

As we explore the many facets of purpose, it becomes easy to forget and important to remember that our focus must remain in the right direction. It is in understanding—to the degree we are able, the Person of God and His character—that we are free to move in the direction of our calling. If we forget Who He is at His core, we will lose the freedom to be our true selves.

For instance, as I was growing up, I had many thoughts of what I would do when I became an adult. Many of them sounded fun, but I assumed they would not be my calling. After all, to serve God, it has to be difficult, right? I don't remember anyone ever actually teaching me that, but in the teachings about sacrifice and laying down selfish ambitions, I had heard the message that in order to really serve God, I had to be miserable.

I'm not sure what God you serve, but that description is certainly not the God I want to serve. No, I haven't started following a different God, but I have grown in my understanding of Who He actually is. As I have learned more about His character, I have found that at the core of His being is a Love we will never fully understand. Out of that Love flows a desire for His beloved to fully experience and enjoy life!

In my mind, one of the most compelling proofs for this belief is our taste buds. We have scientific reason for these sensory nerve endings and their role in the process of digestion, but I like to believe they are for a greater purpose — our enjoyment. If the only reason for food is nourishment and the only reason for taste buds is to make sure our body releases the right chemicals to break down the food, then why create so many different flavors and the mechanism to differentiate and enjoy them? I believe God built many features into His creation, giving us the senses to experience the world around us simply for our pleasure. He wants us to enjoy what He created for us!

So, why should we think that this God, who takes pleasure in our enjoyment of His gifts in creation, wants to sentence us to a lifetime calling we dread being a part of each day? We shouldn't. Does this mean we never have seasons for doing something we'd rather not? No. Does it mean we should follow our wants all the time instead of following His direction? Of course not. But if obedience is truly better than sacrifice as the Bible teaches (1 Samuel 15:22), we must discover what God wants and obey. Sometimes, that path will involve sacrifice, but more often than not, it will also bring great joy and fulfillment, even in those times of sacrifice.

We do ourselves and our God a disservice when we choose the less appealing path simply because we assume that is His choice for us.

Once upon a time, I would not have imagined I could serve God with my life and still enjoy so much what I do. Many people seem to think I live a life of sacrifice because of the path I have chosen in missions, but I cannot imagine anything I would rather do or any life I would choose instead.

One of my favorite chapters of the Bible is Psalm 37. So many of the Psalms are inspiring and many of my go-to passages are in Psalms. But this particular chapter has one of the most famous verses of the whole Bible. Promise boxes, pillows, wall hangings and almost any other medium for scribing Bible verses can be found with this verse etched, stitched or otherwise printed on or in them. Verse 4 states, "Delight yourself in the Lord and He will give you the desires of your heart." I know people who assume this means God is like a cosmic Santa Claus. If you take the time to sit on His lap for a few minutes once a year, you can give Him a list of all the things you want and expect to get at least one or two of them.

I have been reminded on several occasions as I pray about decisions that there is much more to it than that. At times when I'm praying for wisdom concerning a decision or hoping for one outcome or another, I assume I already know the answer. My usual assumption is that God will require me to choose the option I most fear. Often when I think in this manner, it is because I have put my focus on me and have forgotten His character again. I am certainly not delighting in Him since I'm too busy worrying about what I fear will happen.

When I realize I am thinking this way, I repent and get my priorities straight, and then I remember what I believe this verse is really saying. Yes, I do believe it means God will grant us the fulfillment of our deepest desires as we delight in Him, but I am convinced it's more than that. I believe the more we delight ourselves in Him, the more He is able to put HIS desires for us into our hearts, and then He is easily able to fulfill those things because they were His dreams in the first place.

Don't get me wrong here. I don't think God hijacks our dreams and takes over our heart's desires. I believe our desires for success (significance) and family (belonging) — the deepest things we hope for — were built into us from the very beginning, according to the design God had in mind as He formed us. I've found that as I've learned more about myself and my identity in Him, my desires have been refined. Some of the things I previously thought I wanted have faded to nothing, but others have grown into deep passions that my heart cries out to see fulfilled.

As we seek Him and His Kingdom, He can add to us all that we hope for because our hopes and dreams will be His. We will pray for His will and His desires because He will place those in our hearts as well. We can be like King David — in being people after God's heart — because He will make our hearts more like His as we seek Him first. Also like David, we will continue to fail and will still have to battle our sin nature at times, but we will want to overcome in favor of the dreams of God in our lives. We will have the strength to walk forward when we choose, like Jesus, to pray "not my will, but Yours!"

So, as we pray and ask God to show us our purpose, in light of our place as His Beloved, let's keep our eyes fixed on Him above all!

> I've found that as I've learned more about myself and my identity in Him, my desires have been refined. Some of the things I previously thought I wanted have faded to nothing, but others have grown into deep passions that my heart cries out to see fulfilled.

QUESTIONS TO PONDER:

1. What was your idea of the dream job when you were a child?

    _____

    _____

    _____

    _____

    _____

2. How has your understanding of God's character shaped your view of the future?

    _____

    _____

    _____

    _____

    _____

3. What are some things in creation you are thankful you can experience? Your favorite food, perhaps?

    _____

    _____

    _____

    _____

    _____

4. What are your dreams? What do you hope for?

    _____

    _____

    _____

    _____

RECOMMENDED READING:

1. Psalm 37 — Check out the context of the verse we quote so often.

_____

_____

_____

RECOMMENDED ACTIVITIES:

2. Be aware of the things in creation that bring you pleasure and recognize God's design. Thank Him for the gifts in nature that He's given us.

_____

_____

_____

3. Set aside time to dream with God. Write, draw or process in whatever way you are most comfortable, and just dream. Tell God your hopes, and let Him speak His hopes and dreams into you. (I guarantee His hopes are bigger than yours!)

_____

_____

_____

CHAPTER TWELVE

OH, THE POSSIBILITIES!

"Most people live life on the path we set for them, too afraid to explore any other. But once in a while, people like you come along who knock down all the obstacles we put in your way. People who realize free will is a gift that you'll never know how to use until you fight for it. I think that's the chairman's real plan. That maybe one day, we won't write the plan, you will." – The Adjustment Bureau (2011)

I enjoy watching the movie *The Adjustment Bureau* because it illustrates a great picture of the God many people seem to believe in, though many of them would perhaps never admit it. "The Chairman" is the being who plans out every event of every life, and the "Adjustment Bureau" consists of other angel-like beings who make sure things happen according to plan. Their job is to make sure nothing outside the plan occurs and that humans never find out the free will they enjoy is a façade.

As the story unfolds, we discover that even the deaths of the protagonist's father and brother were planned to affect him in a way that moves him into the position the Chairman had originally planned and designed for him. Now, I know of no Christian who would say God orchestrates overdoses or accidental deaths of people to motivate or change others. I have, however, heard explanations like, "We don't understand why, but God has His reasons" spoken to those who are mourning the loss of a loved one. I know those words are meant to bring comfort, but is it really comforting to think God ordains things like sickness, death or destruction to fulfill His purpose for us?

The theological position I accepted throughout my childhood is that God ordains or at least knows everything that will happen. Now, no one told me God causes wars or ordains death or evil. But statements like "God has His reasons" would naturally lead most people to that conclusion if they really thought about it. If God has His reasons for things to happen, then they must be His idea and plan, right? Is there an alternative to that conclusion? Does God really have a reason for the death of a child caused by a drunk driver or the other tragedies that affect our lives?

So, what does this portrayal of God have to do with finding your purpose? Everything! As we talked about in the previous chapter, our view of God affects every decision we make. Unfortunately, some of the widely accepted ideas about the future — and God's knowledge of it — make our involvement in life, through our prayers and our actions, rather insignificant.

That last sentence may not seem true at first, but if God has determined what the future looks like for each of us, and written all of our days down before we show up, do we really have a say in what we do with our lives? Does it matter what we want to do, or should we pray about what path to take if it's already mapped out in a book? Will God send angels and other beings to make sure we stay on course? If we deviate from the planned path, will He intervene? Can we screw up His plan? How free is our will, really?

To answer those questions, I'll tell you what I believe, and you are free to disagree. God does not have a blueprint for how our lives should go. I'm not convinced He knows exactly how they *will* go. In fact, I'm becoming more confident in recent years that He doesn't.

I can hear the outcry even as I write this. "Blasphemy! God knows everything!" Of course He does. God fully knows everything there is to know in and beyond the universe! Everything that exists is known by God fully and completely. The important issue is whether or not a definitive future already exists to be known. The future exists only as possibilities — the infinite number of outcomes determined by human free will — and therefore, God knows the future as such. This is a theological concept known as Open Theism or the open view.[12]

Before I go any further, please know I am not entirely convinced the open view concept is the completely correct view of the totality of God and reality. God is infinitely much greater than any human being will ever totally comprehend, and I strongly believe no one theory will ever explain Him fully. That said, this theory is the one that most resonates within me. In the following pages, I'll explain why and how this belief affects the rest of the content of this book.

Because this is not meant to be a theology book, I will just give the basic idea of the theory as it relates to our topic. In the open view, some aspects of the future are seen as open because they are dependent on the choices and actions of free agents (free will and humans) who have yet to determine them. God knows every possibility and outcome of every choice we could make, but because the choice has not yet been made, the future doesn't yet exist to be known as fact. In a nutshell, we're comparing possibilities to facts.

Some people dispute this idea because they believe it limits or weakens God. I believe the opposite. The open view perspective means God knows every possible choice and every possible outcome of every choice and their subsequent choices and outcomes (much like

---

12   For a more in depth discussion of this, read *God of the Possible* by Gregory A. Boyd.

an infinite domino effect) to be made by every person on the planet throughout history! I cannot fathom the number of possibilities that equals. I am in awe of a God Who not only knows that number but every detail of all the actual possibilities themselves.[13]

This concept was introduced to me in 2001, and it has solidified in my mind and heart over the years because of biblical evidence and my own personal experiences. But before I share those experiences, I want to discuss several biblical stories that point to the idea that God does not know exactly what the future holds — the times when He changes His plans or His mind about what should or will happen, and even the regrets of some of His own choices.

> The open view perspective means God knows every possible choice and every possible outcome of every choice and their subsequent choices and outcomes to be made by every person on the planet throughout history!

The first example is God's regret in making Saul the King of Israel and his eventual removal from that position (1 Samuel 15). Had God exactly known what Saul would choose to do and become when in power, would He regret giving Saul that power? Wouldn't God be as responsible as Saul for the choices he himself made if He put him in that position knowing Saul's exact future choice?

Exodus 32 is another example of God changing His mind. Moses descends Mount Sinai to find the children of Israel have made an idol. God is furious and declares His plan to destroy them. Moses

---

13 A friend did the math. If each person on earth today were to make 1,000 decisions in a day (big or miniscule), the number of stand-alone, possible paths that everyone's lives could take is more than 70,000 times the number of stars in the Milky Way. When you factor in the near-countless *combinations* of what people's different life-paths could be… it's over thirty times the number of grains of sand in the Sahara Desert. God knows that many different outcomes over a span of just two days.

intercedes, and according to verse 14, "the Lord changed His mind about the harm which He said He would do to His people."

I have talked with fellow Christians who say God never actually intended to destroy His people, that God wouldn't do that. Um, remember Noah and the flood (another example of God regretting a decision He made)? I have also heard people say God knew Moses would intercede, so He wasn't actually going to destroy His people, though He stated the intent. If God truly knew, then He bluffed or lied to manipulate Moses into action. If that were true, I

> I would have to rethink if I actually want to serve a God who leads us through manipulation instead of love.

would have to rethink if I actually want to serve a God who leads us through manipulation instead of love.

Of course, I do very much want to serve God, though I can point to times in my own life when it seemed the words I heard Him speak were untrue. For instance, several years ago, I fasted during the month of January for the coming year. I was hoping for God to give me dreams and visions for the new year and possibly beyond. I was praying for someone special to come along to share his life with me. As I prayed one day about a completely unrelated topic, out of the blue, I felt God say I would have a date on Valentine's Day of that year.

Of course, I immediately began to feel anxious because Valentine's was less than a month away. I sent text messages to a couple of friends I trusted and asked if they would pray and ask for confirmation. I didn't tell them what I was praying about, but both came back with responses that God had spoken to them, completely confirming what I was hearing. I tried to discount what I was feeling but felt God wanted me to trust Him. And so, I trusted Him. Valentine's Day came and went that year, and I have yet to go on my first date.

More recently, I experienced a similar situation, except it was a promise much larger than just a date. The fulfillment of this promise would completely change my life. And yet after 21 months of trusting and praying and hoping, God asked me to lay it down and move on.

As I have worked through these disappointments, I have wrestled with understanding what's happened. While we have no guarantee that full understanding will ever come, I have had to fight through the tough questions in order to keep trusting in God. To be honest, the fight still continues at times.

I have come up with three possible explanations for the inconsistencies in my life: 1) God lied to me, 2) I cannot hear God correctly, 3) God intended for things to happen, but the will of others affected the outcomes. All of these possibilities present difficulties, but I cannot live with the first two.

First of all, had God lied, then I could trust nothing else He says, and I must rethink everything I believe of His character. The second is a bit more difficult. If I heard wrong, then I can trust nothing else I hear and must second guess everything I believe God has said to me. Of course it is possible for us as humans to hear what we believe is God and be mistaken.

A friend of mine likes to say, "Who do I think I am to think I can hear God?" My answer is she is a child of God, His Beloved! He wants to speak to us, and if we assume we are not worthy to hear Him, then everything that fills the first half of this book is worthless. Even at the Shepherd/sheep stage of intimacy, we are expected to know the voice of our Shepherd.

So, the issue I have with the the second possiblity is not that I'm above being mistaken, but that God is great enough to make Himself heard. Although I didn't ask for the promise, the promise was given to me. I wrestled with God. I sought godly council and wisdom. I asked for confirmations. I repeatedly laid those promises He spoke back down at His feet, and they were repeatedly handed back to me as confirmed. I then begged God to show me if I was wrong and had simply turned an "I wish" into a "God said." If I am to believe I was mistaken so much that I clung to and hoped for this thing for nearly two years, then I cannot accept that the fault is all mine. It is an indictment as much on God's ability or willingness to make Himself heard clearly and to clear up the misunderstanding as it is on my ability and desire to hear Him.

And so I am left with the third possibility as the best explanation for the situation I found myself wrestling with. I believe God intended this event to happen, and the choices of the parties involved changed the outcome. The wonderful thing about God is He can use anything to bring good in our lives. Because He is not fixed on a future that must happen His way, He is able to anticipate every choice we can make — along with its possible outcomes — and work it into His masterpiece in ways we cannot imagine.

One fact I have yet to mention is that God is all-powerful. He can determine any part of the future He wishes. He has chosen to give us free will, and in most cases, He will not force His hand, but there are things He has decided *will* happen and there is no question they will happen. Jesus said He will return one day, and there is no question He will. If God has decided that something will happen, then there can be no doubt He will bring it about. However, He can also limit Himself and the timing to the involvement of His children.

God's choice to work through our involvement is the reason for this discussion about the nature of reality and God's knowledge of it. If we take to heart the belief that things will happen the way they are supposed to simply because God wants them that way, we can easily abdicate our role in His work. We have the ability, like Moses or Saul, to change the heart and mind of God through our prayers and actions. We have choices to make, and our choices can and will affect the course of history.

God may have a plan that is His best for each of us, but I'm not so sure. Notice the use of the word "plan" here. Up to this chapter, I have referred to "intended outcomes" instead of "plans." That's because to me the word "plan" has connotations of blueprints, plots, maps or prearranged details. However, in one of the most quoted verses in the Bible, Jeremiah 29:11, it states that God knows the plans He has. I don't believe this means a predetermined outline of everything that will happen in our lives. There is no one path necessarily leading to the future and the hope He has for each of us.

I want to clarify this "plan" discussion because as we talk about finding purpose and destiny, I don't want to cause confusion. I believe God has designed each of us with a special destiny and calling. He has given us gifts He hopes we will use for His glory. We will look at stories from the Bible that clearly illustrate God had destinies in mind. For some, He made that destiny known very early in their lives. God has created us with purpose; however, I struggle to accept that He has a prearranged path for exactly how we will get there. In some cases, people never do arrive at the place God intends their journey to take them.

> There is no one path necessarily leading to the future and the hope He has for each of us.

One of the teachings I received years ago revolutionized my idea of God's "plan" for my life. The speaker said, sometimes, God says do A or B. Other times, He asks, "What do you want to do?"

Somewhere along the line, I believed in the idea that God had a plan for my life, and I just had to try not to get off-course. The idea that God would let me choose the direction my life would take, and be okay with either of my options, was totally foreign to me. Suddenly, I felt like I was living in one of those "choose your own adventure" books I used to read. (In case you're not familiar with them, the author provided different options in several places in the book where readers could choose what should happen next. And depending on the choice made, readers were directed to specific pages to continue the story.)

Could I really choose my own adventure? I was taught I had free will and could make my own choices, but could God really be okay with me choosing *either* A or B? While I believe this is often the case, there are limits. Obviously, if A and B lead us in totally opposite directions, and one involves living in sin, God would clearly have an opinion about which direction I should go. Please don't assume I'm telling you to do just whatever you want and assume God is okay with it. It is vital to seek God for wisdom in decisions, but don't be so afraid of the possibility of hearing Him wrong that you are paralyzed to do anything. He may just tell you to use your brain and choose what seems best to you. In that case, He will bless whichever wisely chosen path you opt to walk.

This is what I hear in the opening quote to this chapter. God really does want us to use our brains and be a part of the process of creating a future. The key is to stay focused on Him and delight in Him so the desires of our heart and, therefore, the choices we make are in line with the desires of His heart.

And during times when we don't understand, we just trust. We trust that no matter the outcome of our choices or the choices of others, God can still weave a beautiful masterpiece of our lives. He has promised He will work everything for good to those who love Him and are called to His purposes (Romans 8:28).

> During times when we don't understand, we just trust. We trust that no matter the outcome of our choices or the choices of others, God can still weave a beautiful masterpiece of our lives.

This is easier said than done, but I am learning it's worth the effort. Some days when I am tempted to escape and disappear into a TV show, book or movie, I simply have to repeat to myself I trust God. My heart may be hurting, and that's okay. But instead of running toward options that will simply dull the pain, I want to choose to run to the only One who can heal the hurt. He is also the only One who can bring about an even greater story than the one I expected. He is the Master Storyteller, and the stories He allows us to write with Him are wonderful!

As you continue reading this book, keep in mind that your prayers and actions can affect the story in powerful ways. How you choose to walk out your identity and purpose can change the course of history! In the following chapters, we'll look a bit at the grand story in which we all get to be active participants. And some of the outcomes we can be sure of.

QUESTIONS TO PONDER:

1. Is the open view new to you? What are your thoughts on this theory?

_____

_____

_____

_____

_____

2. How would you feel about applying the "choose your own adventure" idea into your life? Freeing, scary, or perhaps both?

_____

_____

_____

_____

_____

3. Have you ever wrestled with God over a promised event that didn't happen as you expected?

_____

_____

_____

_____

_____

RECOMMENDED READING:

1. *God of the Possible* by Gregory A. Boyd

_____

_____

LIVE

CHAPTER THIRTEEN

THE BIG PICTURE...YOU'RE IN IT!

"I love... I love... I love you. I never wish to be parted from you from this day on." – Mr. Darcy, *Pride & Prejudice* (2005)

Some people like to read the final page of a book before deciding if they will read the whole thing. I guess they have to know if it ends satisfactorily before they commit to seeing how that ending comes about. I am not a fan of this method. I must admit, however, if I am in a particularly intense part of a book, I may flip some pages forward and skim to see if the names of characters I am attached to are still in the story. But never would I want to read the ending without the whole story unfolding first.

I do, however, have an exception. While the entire story of history is not yet told, I have skipped ahead and read the ending. Spoiler alert:

we win! Jesus Christ is victorious, and we, as His Bride, get to celebrate that victory with Him at a marriage celebration for the ages.

So, why am I spoiling the ending of the greatest story ever told for those who haven't read it yet? Because one of the greatest principles I've learned in my time in missions is to begin with the end in mind. Beginning with the end of His story in mind is important, partly because it is a source of hope in times when life is difficult and seems it will forever be that way. When we are hanging by a thread that is beginning to unravel, it is helpful to know we are not destined for an eternity of struggling, but for an abundant life of overcoming.

> Beginning with the end of His story in mind is important, partly because it is a source of hope in times when life is difficult and seems it will forever be that way.

As encouraging as knowing that truth is, identifying the goal is a bigger reason for starting with the end. We must identify the goal and then work backwards to see what must happen in order for that goal to be reached. To figure out what we are meant to be and do, we have to start with the big picture and then begin narrowing it down to our individual parts from there.

I heard a teaching a number of years ago on the three levels of guidance in determining God's direction: God's overarching plan and purpose, a life mission, and the day-to-day leading of God's Spirit in us. Similar to the idea of beginning with the end in mind, we start broad and get narrower. We'll look at the other two levels in chapter 16. The first level is the overarching plan and purpose of God. That is what this chapter is all about.

So, what is the end? What is the big picture?

The end is the eternal life we get to live in the light of His glory. Read Revelation 21–22 for the descriptions of the New Jerusalem. That is the "ending" for everyone whose name is in the Lamb's Book of Life, those who make up the Bride of Christ.

The most striking verse in this passage actually doesn't mention heaven. It is a cry for the Bridegroom to come. "The Spirit and the bride say 'Come!'" (Revelation 22:17). The exciting part of the end is seeing Love face to face! That is part of the reason I believe it's important to know our place as the Beloved, the Bride of Christ. Part of our purpose is to long and call for the return of our Bridegroom; to "never wish to be parted from [Him] from this day on." As we long for His coming, we can also be a part of bringing about the circumstances that allow for His return.

I am the first to admit I don't understand a lot about the Second Coming of Christ. Many believe it may take place at any second. They may be right. I personally think we're not ready for that yet. It states in Matthew 24:14 that the "gospel of the Kingdom shall be preached in the whole world as a testimony to all the nations, and then the end will come." This verse indicates the whole world has to hear the gospel — not only of salvation through Jesus but of the Kingdom — before the end comes. And if the end is being held off until we've accomplished the job, it may be a long while before the Father tells Jesus it's time to come for His bride.

> Anything that we followers of Christ commit our lives to must work toward the fulfillment of the Great Commission. This is the commandment given to every person who chooses to be a follower of Jesus Christ.

As His bride, we can hasten the day of His return by finishing the command He gave us just before He ascended to the right hand of His Father. He tells us in Matthew 28:18–20, "All authority has been given to Me in heaven and on earth. Go therefore and make disciples of all the nations, baptizing them in the name of the Father and the Son and the Holy Spirit, teaching them to observe all that I commanded you; and lo, I am with you always, even to the end of the age."

Anything that we followers of Christ commit our lives to must work toward the fulfillment of the Great Commission. This is the commandment given to every person who chooses to be a follower of

Jesus Christ. It should be our purpose and goal in life to cry for the coming of our Beloved Bridegroom with every word we speak and every action we take.

To see the whole picture, now that we've looked briefly at the ending, we must go back to the beginning. When God created the heavens and earth, He placed a garden in Eden. The garden was the place He put man and walked with him. The instruction given to Adam was to spread out and fill the earth. Oh, and don't eat from that one tree in the middle of the garden.

Unfortunately, we didn't do so well at following all instructions. Man managed to fill the earth, but we messed up on the tree issue. As a result, God didn't see His "plan" to spread out and fill the earth with us fulfilled as He'd hoped. Instead, we spread out and filled the earth without His presence going with us.

From the time of Moses until that of Jesus, God's presence dwelt in an elegant chamber called the Holy of Holies[14] with an elaborate ritual that had to be followed in order for any visitors to leave His presence alive. And then came that wonderfully terrible day when Jesus was temporarily killed, and the curtain separating His dwelling place from the rest of the world was ripped in two from top to bottom. I have heard it said that at the moment the veil was torn, we were free to enter His presence, but I'm not sure that's the point of the torn veil. Instead, our expansive God was once again free to spread out and be among the people He loves so much!

---

14   The Holy of Holies was a cubic room, fifteen feet across, separated from the rest of the tabernacle, and later the temple, by a thick curtain or veil. It was entered only one day a year, the Day of Atonement, by one man. God sat on the Mercy seat on the Ark of the Covenant and could not be seen by anyone who wished to remain alive. This was not His idea of dwelling with His people, but disobedience had necessitated the separation. Exodus 26:33,34; Leviticus 16:2, 16, 17, 20, 23, 27, 33; I Kings 6:16, 7:50, 8:6; I Chronicles 6:49; 2 Chronicles 3:8, 10, 4:22, 5:7; Psalm 28:2; Ezekiel 41:21, 45:3; Hebrews 9:1, 8, 12, 25, 10:19, 13:11.

So, God is free to spread out and fill the earth with His glory. He wants to expand, He wins, and He has purposed to fill the earth! It states in Isaiah 9:7, "Of the increase of His government and peace there will be no end... The zeal of the Lord of hosts will perform this" (NKJV). This is the overarching purpose of God. His Kingdom will forever be increasing, and it is His zeal that will accomplish this. It does not depend on us, but we get to a part of it!

Everything in that last paragraph is awesome. To fully understand how that information points to our purpose, we must look a little more closely at God's intention as originally told to Abraham in Genesis 12 and repeated throughout the New Testament.

"Now the Lord said to Abram, 'Go forth from your country, and from your relatives, and from your father's house, to the land which I will show you. And I will make you a great nation, and I will bless you, and make your name great; and so you shall be a blessing... And in you all the families of the earth will be blessed'" (Genesis 12:1–3).

According to Paul in Galatians 3, the above passage is the true gospel message. Abraham and his offspring (including all believers through Christ) are 1) blessed *in order* to 2) be a blessing *to* 3) *all* families of the earth. God has indeed blessed us — with His presence, the ability to be in relationship with Him, and the thousands of miracles, big and small, that we experience each day. We are great at accepting the blessings, and we often become so accustomed to receiving them, we don't even notice or recognize the Giver of those blessings anymore.

Unfortunately, too often, we are much less skilled in translating our blessings into blessings for others. How often do we look outside of ourselves and really look for ways to be a blessing to others? Do we look for tangible ways to share our talents and treasures with others? What about sharing the greatest treasure we've received with others? I admit I don't always take the time to share the hope and love I have received in Christ with those who need it so desperately, whether in my own backyard or across the globe.

Reaching into the lives of our neighbors on this planet is our privilege, though. God could snap His fingers and make it certain that everyone on the planet knew His name and His teachings, and yet He has chosen, to some degree, to limit Himself to our involvement. It is largely through our partnership with Him — healing the sick, proclaiming His Word, even giving a cup of cold water in His name — that He will be made known and His Kingdom will expand and be established on the earth.

> We are called to pray for God's Kingdom to come and His will to be done here on earth as it is in heaven. We are also called to be a part of that answer.

We are called to pray for God's Kingdom to come and His will to be done here on earth as it is in heaven. We are also called to be a part of that answer. We have a part to play in His story, and we are privileged to be included in seeing God's plans, which were set in motion from the very beginning, become a reality in the present. In the next few chapters, we'll explore a bit of what it might look like for His "kingdom come" to be a reality, even before He comes back.

QUESTIONS TO PONDER:

1. When you think about your daily life, what is the end goal of most of your activities?

_____

_____

_____

_____

_____

_____

_____

2. How have you been a blessing to someone else recently?

_____

_____

_____

_____

_____

_____

3. What are the blessings God has put in your life, and how can you pass them on to bless others?

_____

_____

_____

_____

_____

_____

RECOMMENDED READING:

1. Revelation 21–22

_____

_____

_____

RECOMMENDED ACTIVITIES:

2. Find a practical way to act on your answer to question 3. Then do it.

_____

_____

_____

CHAPTER FOURTEEN

'TIL KINGDOM COME

*"**Your kingdom come.** Your will be done, on earth as it is in heaven."*
– Matthew 6:10

God modeled the opening verse above after how Jesus taught us to pray. Have you ever wondered what you're really asking for when you say those words? What does it really mean for God's kingdom to come? I know many people who believe that in saying these words, we are praying for Christ to return and establish His kingdom to replace the kingdoms of this world, which have resulted all too often in war, poverty, destruction and death. These Christians picture a celestial domain from which God watches the happenings taking place here on earth. To them, His kingdom is a far off thing to be awaited from the midst of this kingdom of darkness where we are stranded for the time being.

We don't have to wait until Christ returns to see His kingdom come to earth. Colossians 1:13 states, "He rescued us from the domain of darkness and transferred us to the kingdom of His beloved Son." Notice the past tense verbs in that verse. We, who have chosen to let Him rescue us, have already been snatched out of the kingdom of darkness. We already dwell in the domain of our heavenly King.

Merriam-Webster online has several definitions for kingdom. One is "the realm in which God's will is fulfilled," another is "a realm or region in which something is dominant." As we live our lives in a way that displays the reign of God and brings about His will, we bring the kingdom of God to earth.

I once heard a sermon titled "Now, but not yet." The theme of the message was we are the children of God, and our access and authority is given to us by our Father. Much as teenagers are able to buy things with the wealth of their parents (subject to the will of their parents), we are given access to the wealth and authority of our Father. We can't "name and claim" what we want anytime we want because the authority is not ours to command our way. We don't yet live in a world where we are full rulers alongside our Father. Not yet!

But the Kingdom is also not a far off idea we have no access to. The Kingdom is *now*. Our Father owns it all, and we have access and authority over things as He gives it to us. We should pray and believe for things and live in such a way that the Kingdom is shown in our lives today. And yet, we should live with the understanding that our authority in this world is still subject to the will of our Father and, at times, with the consequences of our choices and the choices of others. The inheritance is already ours (now), and one day, it will be given fully to us (but not yet).

As I have pondered what it looks like for God's original plan — establishing His kingdom on earth and dwelling with man — to be reality, God has used a couple of my indulgences to show me what that might look like. I mentioned before I enjoy escaping into other places in my mind, and I can easily get sucked into television shows. A recent indulgence in that area has been the BBC's *Merlin*, and as engaging as it is, God has used this entertainment medium to illustrate the idea of a kingdom to me.

Based on the very little knowledge I have of modern monarchies, I know they don't function quite like they used to. Many people besides the king or queen are involved in the governing process. The image portrayed in *Merlin* is quite different. There is the council of advisors, but the monarch is sovereign. If the monarch decides someone should die, that person has no hope of living unless someone else persuades the king otherwise. If a decree is made by the king, no one can speak against it unless they are ready to be parted from their head or, at least, spend some time in the dungeon.

Thankfully, we are not part of a kingdom ruled by Uther Pendragon or Henry VIII. We are citizens in a Kingdom ruled by Love Himself, a Kingdom of justice, of freedom, and of peace. While our Kingdom is infinitely better than fictional Camelot — or even Albion, the prophesied realm, united and at peace under King Arthur — watching Arthur and Merlin work together with others toward the goal of establishing Albion has illustrated to me important concepts about God's Kingdom and my part in it.

> We are citizens in a Kingdom ruled by Love Himself, a Kingdom of justice, of freedom, and of peace.

One of the first details I noticed in the show is how much time Merlin spends simply serving. He serves Arthur, first as a Prince and then as King. His destiny is to fulfill great things and help Arthur build a kingdom of justice, freedom, and all good things. Over the course of five seasons, you watch as Merlin accomplishes quite a number of those great things. And, you also see him polish armor, serve meals, clean, and serve as a pack mule.

The show's timeline from airing season to season also fast-forwards by one year, three years, and who knows how many other lengths of time. I can only assume those missing years were filled with relative peace and no great deeds; otherwise, they would be part of the show.

Merlin, during those years, must have been busy simply being a servant with little relief from the monotony of polishing armor — if life-threatening situations and kingdom near-endings can be a relief.

We are called to great things, but how often do those great things happen in the course of our daily service to our King? Will Fillingham, a pastor and friend of mine, once posed this question:

"Have you ever thought about the servants in John 2:1–12, where Jesus turned water into wine? We all love the miracles of Jesus and seek after the exciting things of the kingdom that bring us goose bumps and tears, but in order for a miracle to happen, someone had to be told what to do. The servants had to step up and fill the water pots, draw the water out and deliver the wine. They were instructed by Jesus' mother to do whatever they were told by her son. Without serving, miracles really can't happen.

"It seems the servants always know the inside scoop as a result. When the wedding attendant was puzzled as to where the 'good' wine came from, the servants sat back and smiled, knowing they had just witnessed the first miracle of Jesus, and they knew what the others did not. Who knows, maybe they even got the first taste of the good stuff! Membership has its privileges. Don't chase after miracles, chase after serving. Seek to serve today and allow Jesus to take care of the miracles in your life."

Not until I read these paragraphs did I think of those servants, especially not in the way described by Will. I read this passage at a time when I was contemplating what it looks like to "serve God," so I'm grateful Will shared his thoughts when he did. As I thought about the picture of servanthood portrayed on *Merlin*, I remembered those servants who witnessed the first miracle of Jesus. I've also wondered how often I've seen great things happen in the lives of those around me through simple acts of service and God's power moving in the seemingly mundane.

Along with the life of a servant comes the unfortunate result of not getting credit for the things you do. Of course, the reason we serve should never be to get praise for our service, but it is always nice to be recognized for our efforts. This is where knowing our own identity and destiny is imperative. When we know beyond any doubt we are doing what we are called to do, we can continue to work and experience fulfillment in that work, whether or not our efforts are ever recognized on earth.

Merlin spends years serving and saving Arthur with no thanks. He can't share with anyone the countless times he has stopped catastrophes or saved lives. He simply continues to serve and save his friends because he knows it is his destiny and he cares about the people he is serving and saving. Even when another person recognizes his work and points out that it must be difficult to do so much with no reward or recognition, he responds, "My friends are safe and well, that is all I require."

I pray that as you and I realize more and more of our gifts and why we have been given them, we will always be fulfilled in our service to the King. Whether it is recognized by those around us or not, we can have joy even in the mundane, knowing we are a part of the miracles Jesus does in the lives of those we touch.

The greatest lessons I've taken away from my time in Camelot are about sacrifice. The theme of sacrifice was woven throughout much of the series, but the episode in which I most clearly saw it is called "The Darkest Hour." The entire episode has sacrifice at the center, and several aspects stuck out to me.

In "The Darkest Hour," a tear is created between the world of the living and the realm of the dead. The rip must be repaired, and for that to happen, a sacrifice must be made. Prince Arthur, intent on sacrificing himself in order to save the people in his kingdom, sets out with his most faithful knights and Merlin.

Merlin, knowing his destiny is to protect Arthur, secretly plans to take Arthur's place when the time comes and sacrifice himself to close the tear between the two worlds. Through a series of events,

Sir Lancelot learns of Merlin's plan. As I watched the episode, the conversation that follows sank deep into my heart.

> <u>Lancelot</u>: *"When we get to the Isle of the Blessed, do you really intend to sacrifice yourself?"*

> <u>Merlin</u>: *"What do you want me to say?"*

> <u>Lancelot</u>: *"I look at you and I wonder about myself. Would I knowingly give up my life for something?"*

> <u>Merlin</u>: *"You have to have a reason. Something YOU care about. Something that's more important than anything."*

At the time I watched this episode, I was in a season of prayer about the different dreams and visions God had given me for my future, my destiny. I had agreed to a ministry opportunity that would consume the next 16 months of my life. It could delay the completion of this book, and it was also likely a romantic relationship would not happen until after my ministry agreement ended. Once again, the promise of marriage and family had been on my mind.

I pray that as you and I realize more and more of our gifts and why we have been given them, we will always be fulfilled in our service to the King.

As I prayed, I began to feel the need to put some of my hopes and promises on the back burner for a time. It felt like all of these things — the ministry opportunity, my dreams for marriage and family, and writing a book — were too much for me to hope for and carry around all at once. I was convinced I did not have the capacity to trust for all of it at the same time. I came to the conclusion that marriage and family must sit on the shelf for a while, even buried and then resurrected when the time was right.

I wasn't happy with the idea because the more I thought about it, the more I felt like I was putting "life" on the back burner in order to focus on "ministry." Out of nowhere, this *Merlin* episode came to mind, and I realized it felt like I was sacrificing my life in order to fulfill my destiny. I began to think about what it was that was so important to Merlin he would be willing to sacrifice himself in place of the prince, and it hit me: he believed so much in the kingdom Arthur was destined to build that it was worth any cost he had to pay to make sure that kingdom was established.

I wrestled for a while with whether I believed enough not only in the Kingdom but also in the One building it to give my life or whatever else was required of me to see that Kingdom established. I decided it was totally worth it to lay down my life for my King and His Kingdom. I may never be asked to lay down my physical life, but that would be worth it, too. The privilege of playing a small part in the Kingdom that God is establishing on this planet is worth sacrificing everything!

> I decided it was totally worth it to lay down my life for my King and His Kingdom. The privilege of playing a small part in the Kingdom that God is establishing on this planet is worth sacrificing everything!

A warning to those who've not seen *Merlin* but want to: SPOILER! The story didn't end the way Merlin intended. He saved Arthur, but in the end, it was Sir Lancelot who made the sacrifice. He, too, found something important enough to give his life for — the future queen, Arthur's bride-to-be. He loved her, and she had asked that he make sure Arthur came back to her.

I thought about the story's ending as well and realized that maybe my sacrifice would also be for the Bride. Merlin was willing to give himself, but that was not his destiny. Maybe I am more like Lancelot and will actually lay down my "life" for the Kingdom AND for Christ's Bride. After all, I know my primary calling is to the Body/Bride of Christ.[15]

---

15   More on this in Chapter 18.

So, it was settled. I would lay aside the dreams I had for myself, my life and family. I would continue to hope in Jesus for my future — whatever it looked like — and pray I would bring glory to my King as I worked toward His Kingdom come and His will be done on earth as it is in heaven. I knew no matter how difficult it seemed at the time, it would be worth any sacrifice to do my part in bringing about the Kingdom. After all, as Merlin said when he offered to take Arthur's place, "What is the life of a servant compared to that of a [King]?"

Fast forward a few weeks to when I was in a major funk for no apparent reason. I finally carved out time with Jesus to sort through what was going on with me. As I wrote in my journal, I began to notice a theme interwoven throughout the different topics that arose: I felt rejected and completely unimportant. Normally, when a theme like that is present across all of my circumstances, it's a safe bet I am projecting that thought from a much deeper root — my perception of God at that moment.

As I began to ask God why I believed He thought I was so unimportant (when I knew is a lie), it hit me; I talked myself into that belief! In all of my noble, sacrificial thoughts of laying my life down to see His Kingdom established, I had convinced myself that I was disposable. The sentiment of my self-denial was sincere and noble, but God showed me I had taken it too far. The words I felt Him say to me were, "A king is nothing with a bunch of walking dead… My Kingdom is one of abundant life. It's not all about giving up your life for the sake of my Bride; it's about being my Bride!"

Once again I was brought back to the first half of this book, reminded that I am His Beloved. I was reminded that any sacrifice or service I do must flow out of the relationship I have with my King. It is so easy to lose sight of who we are, but our identity must remain the foundation of all that we do! The Kingdom of God is built by those who are fully alive in service to their King, not by those who have decided they are expendable and sacrifice their dreams for the glory of their King. In fact, we cannot fully glorify Him if we are not living out the joy of being His and dreaming with Him!

This does not mean sacrifice won't be involved in serving our King and building the Kingdom. We must count the cost and take up our cross daily, but that does not mean living without hope for what God has in store. The key is to live open handed before God and let Him have everything, trusting that He is good no matter what. Sometimes, we may end up in a situation like Abraham[16] in which God provides a way out of the sacrifice at the last minute. Other times, we may be called to carry the cross all the way to Calvary, but we can still hope because God is the God of resurrection and restoration. Whatever the cost, it is worth it!

As citizens of this incredible Kingdom, everything we do should be in the service and under the reign of our King. This earth is our temporary home, and while it is currently not the ideal it started out as, we can be a part of restoring it to its intended glory. In the next chapter, we'll look at how we can do that.

---

16 In Genesis 22, you can read the story of God's request of Abraham to sacrifice his son, Isaac, and the provision of a ram to take Isaac's place on the altar.

QUESTIONS TO PONDER:

1. What does you serving your King in your life right now look like?

    _____

    _____

    _____

    _____

    _____

    _____

2. For what or whom would you lay down your life? (Don't just write the Kingdom/King because that's Merlin's answer.) More than anything else, what is most important to you?

    _____

    _____

    _____

    _____

    _____

    _____

3. Have you laid down your "life" for something? Have you had an Abraham sacrifice experience in which God provided you a way out?

    _____

    _____

    _____

    _____

    _____

    _____

RECOMMENDED READING:

1. John 2:1–12

_____

_____

_____

RECOMMENDED ACTIVITIES:

2. Seek out a way to serve someone. Then ask God to move through you.

_____

_____

_____

CHAPTER FIFTEEN

SERVING GOD IN EVERYTHING

*"**Whatever you do,** do your work heartily, as for the Lord rather than for men."* – Colossians 3:23

The mental picture I had of heaven was one of the reasons I spent much of my life believing the Kingdom of God was something far off and out of my reach. I thought "heaven" was synonymous with "Kingdom of God," and my understanding of that was Christians sitting around on clouds singing worship songs. I'm not sure where that idea came from, but I pictured heaven as an eternal Sunday morning type worship service.

BORING!

Don't get me wrong; I'm a musician. I love to sing and to worship God! He deserves to be worshiped and glorified by all of creation for all of eternity. However, I've expanded my view of what worship can look like, and I think that broader view has changed my idea of what awaits us and what is truly meant by the phrase "Kingdom of God."

I don't claim to have a full understanding of heaven or what the Kingdom of God looks like, but to explain my current understanding, we must think back to the beginning of man's existence. Think with me for a moment about the Garden of Eden and the first mention of God's idea to create man. "Then God said, 'Let Us make man in Our image, according to Our likeness; and let them rule over the fish of the sea and over the birds of the sky and over the cattle and over all the earth, and over every creeping thing that creeps on the earth'" (Genesis 1:27).

Notice God did not say let Us make man to sing songs to Us forever. A major reason He created us was to have relationship with us. He was so fulfilled in loving and having relationship between the members of the Trinity that He wanted to bring more people into that relationship. However, as it states in Genesis, He also made us to rule with Him. He gave Adam a job: to cultivate the earth.

As we work alongside God, we can bring Him glory and worship Him with our work as much as with our words.

Many people believe work was a result of the fall of man into sin, but Adam was given his job *before* he disobeyed. The consequence of sin was the work would be hard and yield less than the best. Therefore, since work was not a product of man's disobedience, I believe we will continue to work in the life to come. We were made to fellowship with God *and* rule and work with Him. As we work alongside God, we can bring Him glory and worship Him with our work as much as with our words.

Many Christians have lost this perspective because of our view of the world during the week as opposed to our view of Sunday morning (or whichever day your weekly worship service is held). We see that weekly celebration time with the Body of Christ as the part of our week that belongs to God. The rest of the week is the "secular" or "worldly" part of our week.

In contrast, people are not only citizens of a kingdom when they are present in the court of the king. They are subject to the king (and aware of their submission) at all times during their life and work.

Centuries before the birth of Christ, Plato presented philosophies which influenced and shaped the way many people have thought about the world throughout the subsequent millennia. One such philosophy is the Secular-Sacred split. It is a dichotomy[17] — "a division into two especially mutually exclusive or contradictory groups or entities." In modern thinking (which, in reality, is ancient and inherited from Plato and his contemporaries), anything related to the physical world belongs on one side of the split — the secular, and everything related to the supernatural belongs on the other side — the sacred.

This tends to be the view of the Church in the areas of civilization influenced heavily by Greco-Roman philosophies. In general, there is the holy day each week where we go to church and spend at least part of the day thinking about God. The rest of the week falls into the secular category where we go to school or work, grocery shop and do all the non-spiritual aspects of our lives. This is not how things were viewed in the Old Testament, and I don't believe it's how God sees it either.

One of my favorite teachings comes from a woman named Landa Cope, who wrote a book called the *Old Testament Templates*. In her book, she points out that God taught Israel how to succeed in every area of life. The commands He set forth in the law were not all about how to worship Him. That was a part of it, but He also taught them how to stay healthy. Much of what He taught the Israelites through the law can act as a template for discipling nations even today. He taught them principles for every area of their society — from worship to health and sanitation, from representative government to debt and loans.

---

17   "Dichotomy." *Merriam-Webster.com*. Merriam-Webster, n.d. Web. 11 Jan. 2016.

Every society creates spheres of influence that help to shape it, and God gave instructions in His Word that teach us His principles for each sphere. I'm beginning to hear more and more people in the Church talk about these spheres of society. These areas include government, family, education, economics (including research & development, production & sales), science & technology (including health & wellness), celebration (including sports, entertainment, arts), media (including journalism, social media, internet), and religion.

Often we in the Church see only the area of religion — whether it's local churches, missions, or religious organizations — as the sphere of society that we have influence over, our sphere of influence. We let the "world" influence the other spheres, such as science or entertainment, because they are secular and, therefore, not our concern. We focus our energy on trying to bring people into our circle instead of going outside our sphere and taking our influence to other areas of society. Even in missions, we often go to the far reaches of the earth with the intention of establishing the Church and sharing Christ's love, thereby, influencing the religion sphere of that society. But we make no effort to reach into the other areas of their lives (e.g., family, government, education, etc.).

As we discussed in chapter 13, Matthew 24:14 states the "gospel *of the Kingdom* shall be preached in the whole world as a testimony to all the nations, and then the end will come" (emphasis mine). It's not the gospel of salvation alone that must be preached. I have met people who think that as soon as we have handed a tract to every person or transmitted the gospel over the internet and airwaves in every area of the planet, Jesus will come back. There is so much more to the gospel than that! It is the gospel of the KINGDOM. A kingdom is a society, and as such, every sphere of society is a part of that kingdom.

Let's also look at Matthew 28:18–20 again: "All authority has been given to Me in heaven and on earth. Go therefore and *make disciples* of all the nations, *baptizing them* in the name of the Father and the Son and the Holy Spirit, *teaching them to observe all that I commanded you;* and lo, I am with you always, even to the end of the age" (emphasis mine).

A great amount of this command deals with the religious area of life. We are called to baptize people. That's certainly a religious activity, and there must be evangelism and other spiritual aspects of the process even before baptism, but what of the other half of the command? In my opinion, teaching people to observe ALL that I commanded would include the principles for every other area of life as well. Principles of ethical business and prevention of illness are important and no less part of the truth than the grace that Jesus offers.

Everyone who considers himself or herself a follower of Jesus is called to be a part of this process of spreading the Kingdom of God throughout the earth as part of the Great Commission. However, that doesn't mean we are all called to go to a village in Africa and preach salvation to the people there. It is an awesome thing to serve God in the sphere of religion full time. It is also an awesome thing to serve God in Hollywood, bringing His truth to the entertainment industry, which greatly influences our society and everyone else around the world. It is equally awesome to own and operate a business with integrity and morality, or to teach the next generation the principles that will bring more of the Kingdom of God to the world. We spread the kingdom of God through influencing religion, family, government, education, to name a few spheres, and by sharing and implementing the principles of God in each area.

> We spread the kingdom of God through influencing religion, family, government, education, to name a few spheres, and by sharing and implementing the principles of God in each area.

Think about the people we read about in the Bible. David operated in the sphere of government. Luke was a physician. Lydia, a woman Paul baptized in Acts 16, was a saleswoman, involved in the economic sphere. Mary was a stay-at-home mom. Jesus didn't ask Peter to stop being a fisherman. He simply offered to show him how to catch a new kind of fish. The only people made to leave their "worldly" occupation were those whose profession involved sin.

One of the first examples that comes to mind when I think about this split between the sacred and secular is music. I'm going to offend some people, but one of my greatest pet peeves is "Christian" music. Most of it sounds like a poor imitation of what "the world" originally created. I'm generalizing, of course. I do enjoy listening to several Christian bands, and I love the message they present in their music. However, listening to Christian radio drives me crazy because many of the songs fit into the popular but "poor imitation of the original" classification.

Our God is the Creator of the universe! Shouldn't we as His followers — made in His image and temples of His Spirit — be among the most creative people in every sphere, on the cutting edge of every domain in our society, instead of simply putting our own spin on the world's originals?

> Shouldn't we as His followers — made in His image and temples of His Spirit — be among the most creative people in every sphere, on the cutting edge of every domain in our society, instead of simply putting our own spin on the world's originals?

Then we have bands made up of followers of Jesus who want to influence the secular music scene. I have heard them ripped apart by Christians who think it's wrong to be a part of "the world" in that way. My question to these Christians is, "If we, as followers of Jesus, cannot or will not influence the world, how can we complain about how bad the world is getting?"

God has given each of us gifts to use to bring His Kingdom to earth, and if we try to keep all of those gifts within the sphere of religion, we are depriving the world of so much of what God wants to pour into it. We ought to strive to be at the forefront of every sphere in our society and show that the principles of God work in every area of modern life.

The other side of this coin is demonstrated when we throw ourselves into affecting other spheres without bringing along the spiritual element. A hugely debated hot topic in the Church, and the world at large right now, is human trafficking. My heart aches for the children, women and men who are caught up on all fronts of this issue. We must rise up and change the situation! However, if we buy girls out of prostitution and send them on their way without giving them the hope that only comes from God, we have not rescued them. If we give them nothing to move toward, many of them will simply go back to what they know. In some cases, children are returned to their families only to be re-sold into slavery by their parents again.

Many churches, mission agencies and non-profit organizations are using platforms and channels outside the sphere of religion to affect change. Digging wells, teaching English, health education, and a myriad of other opportunities are available all across the globe. However, none of these good deeds will ever solve all the problems this world faces. Billions of dollars have been poured into African nations in hopes of stopping the horrible social and economic issues that plague this continent. But it will never work. Not until we bring the Spirit and Truth of God to change the hearts of people will good deeds fix the problems of human trafficking, slavery, poverty, sickness, starvation, war, and all the other problems facing our world.

We must avoid the extremes of trying to influence only the sphere of religion or influencing other spheres of society without the Truth of God's Word if we want to fulfill the commission we've received and hasten the day of our Bridegroom's return. We cannot separate the physical from the spiritual. We must meet the physical needs of the world's population *while* offering them the hope that can only come from beyond this world — the spiritual. We need people who are skilled in all areas of society to share their knowledge and talents with others and help them to know God at the same time. As the Church, we must reach beyond the walls of our building and our "religion" and live an integrated life where the Spirit is allowed access to every aspect of life and culture.

As each of us finds a sphere in which we can excel and gain influence, *living* integrated lives that use all aspects of life as ways to glorify God, only then can we be the conduit of God's truth and blessing in every area of society. The world is longing for a God who will come and meet them in the midst of life, not in the midst of a certain building. Let's introduce the world to our God, who cares about the state of their spiritual life *and* the everyday physical world that abounds around them.

I have heard it said of some people that they are "so heavenly minded, they are of no earthly good." They spend their days so focused on the far away idea of heaven that they are oblivious to the ways they could bring God's kingdom to earth — today. With their heads in "the clouds," nothing on earth matters to them. Let's not be one of those people! I must also admit that at times, I've thought environmentalists, or "bunny-huggers" as I first heard them called, have gone overboard. I have believed their claims to be downright ridiculous; however, we have been given this place to steward, and many of us don't do it very well. Some people even hold to the idea that this world will all burn one day anyway, so as long as we're getting people saved, all is well. This, too, is the wrong attitude. As followers of the One who created the world, we should be leading the way in preserving and caring for it.

One Christmas, as I prayed about the previous year and the one to come, God told me "heaven will look different because of your time on earth." Wow. I'm not sure I will ever get my mind completely into the idea that I can affect the landscape of heaven. So I'm not sure if that message means people I've influenced will be there, or if there is some other way I'm affecting heaven. Suffice it to say, you and I have a part to play in building the Kingdom on earth that can, in some way, shape the Kingdom for eternity! If that doesn't motivate you to be a world-changer, I'm not sure what will.

As we discover the purpose we were made for and walk in that purpose for the glory of God, the Kingdom will be established on earth. God is in the process of restoring and renewing this world, and everything we do here and now can be a part of that renewal. So, let's begin to ask God to reveal who He made us to be and what spheres of society and the world we can influence, through glorifying Him, and how we can bring His Kingdom to earth.

QUESTIONS TO PONDER:

1. How do you see the dichotomy of the secular/sacred split operating in your own life?

_____

_____

_____

_____

_____

_____

_____

_____

_____

_____

_____

2. Is there a sphere of society you are especially drawn to be a part of and to influence?

_____

_____

_____

_____

_____

_____

_____

_____

_____

_____

_____

3. How would you affect your life if you began to treat every aspect of it as being as important as the "sacred"?

_____

_____

_____

_____

_____

_____

_____

_____

_____

_____

_____

_____

_____

RECOMMENDED READING:

1. *Heaven is a Place on Earth* by Michael E. Wittmer

_____

_____

_____

2. *The Book That Transforms Nations* by Loren Cunningham

_____

_____

_____

LIVE
CHAPTER SIXTEEN

TURN, TURN, TURN

"To everything there is a season, and a time to every purpose under heaven." – Ecclesiastes 3:1 (NKJV)

I loved living in Colorado. Having grown up in Florida, I spent most of my childhood not knowing the wonder of the seasons. Well, perhaps not completely. We had a few days a year of cooler temperatures. That broke up our seasons of hot/humid and hurricanes. In Colorado, though, you can experience a real winter, spring, summer and autumn most years. I love different aspects of each season, and I'm almost always ready for one to end and the next to begin — although, some excite me more than others.

Like geographic areas, life also experiences seasons. And each has a variety of wonders to offer. Some seasons bring growth and new beginnings; others bring opportunities for adventure and fun. Some bring rest and refreshment and others a time of pain and death. No matter what each season brings, each has its own beauty if we are willing to see it.

This has become more evident to me in the last few years. God has always spoken to me through sunsets; however, I am mostly a morning person. I love to watch the sun rise and turn the mountains pink and purple, but a beautiful sunrise rarely speaks to my heart of God and His love for me like a sunset. One evening as I was watching a particularly magnificent display of orange and purple over the mountains, I asked God why this part of nature shouts so loudly to me. The answer was surprising and a bit terrifying.

He told me He speaks more clearly of His love through sunsets because He wants me to be aware of the beauty that can be seen, even in the midst of coming darkness. It is not only the dawn that brings beauty, but the "dark night of the soul" offers its beauty even in the midst of the pain and uncertainty if only we will be aware of it.

> There are seasons that seem totally dark with no moonlight or even stars to break the blackness. But the remembered beauty of the fading light and the promise of the coming dawn are always there, bringing hope that this, too, shall pass.

Eventually, all the colors fade into darkness, and of course, the sunset doesn't last all night. There are seasons that seem totally dark with no moonlight or even stars to break the blackness. But the remembered beauty of the fading light and the promise of the coming dawn are always there, bringing hope that this, too, shall pass.

Every season passes eventually, and as we breathe a sigh of relief or grieve its passing, we must also be willing to move forward with the next season of our life. So many people try to live in either the past or the future and miss out on so much of the right now. And yet without the right now, the past and the future lose some of their significance and promise. It is often the things learned in the right now that make the past and future special.

I can think of biblical heroes who were given a glimpse of what was to come, so they tried to live in the future before they were ready. Moses tried to deliver a Hebrew slave from his oppressor. But instead of becoming a deliverer he became a murderer. It was only after 40 years of learning to shepherd and care for sheep in the backside of the wilderness that he was ready for his destiny. And I have a suspicion that if he had gone into that season of being a shepherd, thinking of any future glory, he would not have learned what he needed to and become the man and leader he eventually was.

Joseph is another example of a man who went through many seasons before his destiny was realized. He saw himself, in a God-given dream, as someone his family would bow to. And the next thing he knew, he was being trafficked as a slave to Egypt. He began to gain respect and responsibility, thriving in his position of slavery only to find himself falsely accused and in prison. He begins to do well in the prison, makes a "friend," and then is forgotten as soon as the guy is free.

Poor Joseph can't catch a break it seems. Each time the dawn appears to be coming, darkness descends again. And yet, he remains faithful to God in every season, engaged in his daily challenges and decision instead of longing for something else, and learning the skills necessary to fulfill his purpose with integrity and excellence. He is an incredible example of being faithful to God in every season. He is the depiction of the word I find myself appreciating and hating at the same time: waiting.

For the most part, I am a patient person. Waiting in a line doesn't typically bother me too much. I get rather impatient, however, when I'm going to be late for an appointment. The exception to this virtue seems to be waiting for the timing of God. As I have walked my journey with Him, I too have seen glimpses of the woman He has designed me to be and the glorious things He is preparing me to do. Like Joseph, I have probably opened my mouth a bit more than was prudent. Did he really think his family wanted to hear about his dream that they would all bow to him? And like Joseph, I have found myself waiting far longer than I would like at times to see the completion of my dreams. I have found myself asking — along with Rapunzel from Disney's *Tangled* — "when will my life begin?" Thankfully, my waiting isn't happening in a tower, in prison, or as a slave.

As much as I hate the waiting process, I am learning the value of it. So much can be learned and accomplished in the seasons of waiting. It is in those seasons we can develop the character that prepares us for the season of release and promise we are waiting for. It is the seasons of waiting and hardships that build the integrity necessary for the successes to come.

Many people think character is synonymous with morality. The idea is that as long as you are moral in your business ethics or life, you have good character. That is certainly part of it, but it's not the whole picture. In his book titled *Integrity*, Dr. Henry Cloud defines character as "the ability to meet the demands of reality."

"Life has a lot of realities: relational, market pressures, internal realities, problems and obstacles, moral realities and others. The mature character is able to meet the demands of those realities and be fruitful in the midst of them.[18]" Dr. Cloud uses the illustration of a tree bearing fruit. A person's character is the tree, and the fruit they bear is the result of their character — skills, talents, courage, perseverance, moral/ethical code, operating out of love vs. selfishness, trustworthiness, and so on. If "the tree" is good, the fruit will be good.

Likewise, integrity is often defined as honesty. A businessman who operates an honest business without cheating people is said to be a person of integrity. Once again, that is only a part of the picture. The actual definition[19] is "firm adherence to a code of especially moral or

---

18   http://www.cloudtownsend.com/introduction-to-character/

19   "Integrity." *Merriam-Webster.com.* Merriam-Webster, n.d. Web. 11 Jan. 2016.

artistic values: incorruptibility; an unimpaired condition: soundness; the quality or state of being complete or undivided: completeness."

So in order to have integrity and character, we must be whole or complete and able to meet reality's demands. This is where our waiting process comes into play. If God were to allow us to arrive at His grand destination for us at the beginning of our journey, we would most likely be of no use to Him or anyone else. Just as babies have to grow and learn, adults who will reach the level of integrity and character to be used by God must continue that process long after they're "grown up." It is in the place of waiting that we learn and strengthen the aspects of our character that will make us successful and develop the integrity to handle any success we achieve.

> The seasons of waiting have also taught me waiting is not synonymous with twiddling our thumbs.

The seasons of waiting have also taught me waiting is not synonymous with twiddling our thumbs. Joseph spent his seasons of waiting working, and doing so with excellence. It was the work Joseph did and his attitude in the midst of that work that grew his character and integrity needed for the future season of success. If he had simply sat around "waiting" for his big break to come, it likely never would have. And if it had, Egypt and the surrounding nations may have starved to death.

Colossians 3:23 states, "Whatever you do, do your work heartily, as for the Lord rather than for men." It is certainly easier to do work with excellence when we see the value in it or feel successful. During the seasons in which Joseph was feeding people who would have starved without his aid, it must have been easy and rewarding to be diligent and excellent in his work. However, he would not have risen to that position without the seasons of scrubbing toilets in Potiphar's house or in prison. So, wherever we find ourselves, we must do all we are given to do with excellence and observe what we can learn from every season.

Another important thing to realize about seasons is that God's grace is sufficient for us to walk through each and every one of them. His grace is more than enough; it is abundant. But every season has its end. At times, it's easy to get so comfortable in one season that we want to camp out for longer than we should. I have found that when a season in my life is ending, grace begins to lift.

When I lived in Afghanistan, the stares of men drove me a little crazy at times, but God gave me special grace to bear it while I was in that culture. However, as the time for me to leave was nearing, and I began lamenting not wanting to go, the grace lifted significantly. The last few days before I left, the simple occurrence of being ogled became so annoying I had to physically restrain my right arm at one point because I caught it moving, preparing to give one guy a black eye through which to stare at me. By the time I left, I couldn't wait to be done with that aspect of the culture. The men hadn't just started staring more intently, but my grace to deal with it was gone.

> His grace is more than enough; it is abundant. But every season has its end. I have found that when a season in my life is ending, grace begins to lift.

That is a simple example of how God can move us out of a place where we have become too comfortable. There is grace for everything we are called to walk through. If you are in a place where you just can't deal with it anymore, perhaps it's time to ask God if He is trying to move you elsewhere. Of course, the answer may be you need to develop some aspect of your character, and you're in one of those times of testing we all love so much. In the case of seasons of testing, rather than removal, you must be open to hear God say you are meant to be right there, and then allow Him to give you grace for that season. Although, the answer may be you have become too comfortable, and God is trying to get you to move elsewhere.

Seasons are also a part of our relationships and spheres of influence. I can look back at my life and see when I had a certain friend I assumed would be my best friend forever, and yet we never communicate anymore. Our lives have taken different paths, and we simply don't intersect anymore. Neither path was wrong, but our season of common interests and lifestyles has passed.

Of course, we'll have friends who stay with us forever and no amount of time or distance seems to alter the relationship, but those are rare. As people experience life changes, it is natural to find others in similar circumstances to relate to, those who understand our current stage of life.

I underscore this point simply to say it is not failure when some friendships fade over time. Some people are meant to be part of our lives for a season to build up and encourage. If someone leaves a wake of wounded people behind him or her, obviously that is a different issue. But it is normal for people to lose touch as seasons change and life takes different paths. I am thankful for the friends I have had throughout my life and the richness they have brought into it along each step of my journey.

The changes seasons bring in our relationships go beyond friendships, too. In some seasons, people are called to a certain sphere of influence, and in other seasons, they no longer fit there. For example, couples who have been married for 25 years are probably not the best choice to lead a singles' ministry. Conversely, in my current state of singleness, I'm probably not the ideal speaker for a marriage or parenting retreat. We have to be willing to follow God into new spheres of influence as we walk the journey with him, understanding that giving up leading the youth group or singles' ministry after 30 years isn't failure, but simply a new season.

The calling God has on each one of us spans our lifetime, but it may look differently in each season. I mentioned in chapter 13 the three levels of guidance we can look to as we walk this journey. They are God's overarching plan and purpose, a life mission, and the day-to-day leading of God's Spirit in us. We have already talked about the Word and overarching plan of God in chapters 13 through 15, in which I discuss how we are all called to be a part of bringing His Kingdom.

The remaining two levels of guidance will be covered very briefly. The reason for this jump is while God's end goals apply to every citizen of His kingdom, the two subsequent levels are different for each one of us. I can't tell you what your life mission is, or what it will look like in every season you go through. I wish I knew what my own mission will look like in the seasons I have yet to walk through. However, I share briefly what the levels are and give examples from the life of the Apostle Paul to illustrate the ideas.

The second level is a life mission. Paul's life mission was to take the gospel of Jesus to the Gentiles (Romans 15:16). Everywhere he went and all he did worked toward that goal. He didn't always know which direction he would go next, but he knew wherever he ended up he must tell the Gentiles of their acceptance into the family of God.

We then end the discussion on guidance levels with the daily leading of the Spirit. As we seek to keep the lines of communication open between the Spirit and us, He will guide us. In Acts 20, Paul speaks of being compelled by the Spirit to go to Jerusalem. On two other occasions he attempted to go to Asia, but the Spirit prevented him from going. Instead, Paul received the call to Macedonia. You may have examples from your own life.

These levels of guidance may appear to conflict with chapter 12, which speaks against the idea of a blueprint for our lives. However, I believe there are times in life when God has a specific place where He knows we would be effective in building His Kingdom or even be an answer to someone's prayer. As much as I disagree with the thought that God has every step and event of our lives planned out, He is still God and He is still sovereign and all-powerful. He has the authority and freedom to step in and redirect our steps if He chooses, but we still have the choice of whether or not to follow His direction.

As we work toward achieving the goals of God, walking in the calling and gifts He has given us, He will guide our steps. Don't be afraid to move into a new season with God simply because it's different than what you've done so far. Writing a book and teaching are very different than the many other things I've done, but they still work toward the goal of bringing the Kingdom and ministering to the Body, and so they fit with my calling.

In whichever season you find yourself walking right now, find things to do and do them with excellence. Let God build your character and integrity for the next seasons to come. Enjoy the people in your life right now and cherish the time you have with them, knowing they may not be around forever. If they are the iron God is using to sharpen you, thank God for them. Enjoy the journey with God and allow Him to pour His grace into every season through which you travel.

> As we work toward achieving the goals of God, walking in the calling and gifts He has given us, He will guide our steps. Don't be afraid to move into a new season with God simply because it's different than what you've done so far.

We are not the first ones to walk this journey of relationship with Jesus. In the next chapter, we will look at the stories of some of my heroes. We'll look at their journeys as they discover who God made them to be and why. Perhaps their stories will give us hope and courage to continue our own journeys and to discover why in heaven we're on earth.

QUESTIONS TO PONDER:

1. What is your favorite season of the year? Why?

_____

_____

_____

_____

_____

2. Have you experienced a season of waiting? What were you waiting for? What did you learn?

_____

_____

_____

_____

3. What is the most difficult part of transitioning into a new season? What is the best part?

_____

_____

_____

_____

RECOMMENDED READING:

1. Genesis 37–50 — The story of Joseph

_____

_____

2. *Integrity* by Dr. Henry Cloud

_____

_____

CHAPTER SEVENTEEN

THOSE WHO'VE GONE BEFORE

"We, today, stand on the shoulders of our predecessors who have gone before us. We, as their successors, must catch the torch of freedom and liberty passed on to us by our ancestors." – Benjamin E. Mays

Although the above quote refers to the freedom and liberty of a nation, our heroes of the faith have passed on a type of freedom that is much more global and eternal — the freedom to walk in who we were made to be. With their stories, they have left us awesome examples of inspiration. They show us the process of accepting one's true identity. In their lives, we can see images of discovering and living with a purpose. In this chapter, I discuss a few of my favorite Bible heroes' stories, and hopefully by standing on their shoulders, we can see more clearly the destiny God has in mind for us.

Gideon is one of my favorite people in the Bible. I identify with him and his actions in many ways, most of which are found in the early part of his story. When we first meet Gideon in Judges 6, he is hiding, cowering even. Israel has been severely oppressed by the Midianites, and Gideon is beating wheat in a wine press, trying to save even the smallest scrap of food.

As he tries to stay out of sight, an angel appears and says, "The Lord is with you, O valiant warrior." Gideon phrases his response much better than I would have, 'Are you crazy? How can you say God is with us? Have you seen what's going on around here? He brought us out of Egypt just to leave us here to die.'

> The first sentence God speaks to Gideon is one of identity! He doesn't berate Gideon for hiding; He calls him out of hiding by calling out who he was created to be. The greeting doesn't match where Gideon is in life but where God wants to take him.

The angel then responds, "Go in this your strength and deliver Israel from the hand of Midian. Have I not sent you?" And here is perhaps the part of Gideon's story that I relate with more than any other. Judges 6:15 (MSG) says, "Gideon said to him, 'Me, my master? How and with what could I ever save Israel? Look at me. My clan's the weakest in Manasseh and I'm the runt of the litter.'"

The story continues and Gideon does, indeed, deliver Israel from Midian. There are many incredible parts of his story, and we'll look at some of them as we go. I want to pause here because the beginning of his story is always the most fascinating to me. The first sentence God speaks to Gideon is one of identity! He doesn't berate Gideon for hiding; He calls him out of hiding by calling out who he was created to be. The greeting doesn't match where Gideon is in life but where God wants to take him.

When God tries to call out our identity and destiny, many times we respond like Gideon, asking God just how crazy He must be to say such things to us. We throw our circumstances in God's face as proof that He must be mistaken at the very least if not crazy. Then, just in case our circumstances aren't enough to convince God of His mistake, we add in the lies we believe about ourselves to prove once and for all He must have the wrong person.

As the story goes on, the angel sticks around at Gideon's request to perform a sign to prove he is truly an angel of God. I love that. Often, when I am struggling to accept what God has said, I feel like it's against the rules to ask for "a sign" to prove it's truly Him. I'm not sure where it comes from, but in my mind, the idea has been planted that questioning and asking for signs from God shows a lack of faith. Yet Gideon, the valiant warrior and deliverer of Israel, asks for and receives specific confirmation on multiple occasions. Not only did God not scold him for a lack of faith, but also He granted his requests. That is encouraging to me!

As Gideon's story continues into chapter 7 of Judges, the time for battle arrives. Gideon has torn down the altar of Baal and replaced it with one to God. He has received his second and third confirmations that he truly is God's choice to deliver Israel, and it is time to walk in that destiny. He has gathered 32,000 men to fight with him, but God is not a fan of this army.

Knowing Israel's tendency to take credit away from God and forget all He does for them, God asks Gideon to decrease the army's numbers so no doubt remains the victory belongs to God alone. When told all who are scared are dismissed, the army shrinks to 10,000, but that is still not acceptable to God. So he whittles the number down to 300 who lapped water like dogs. Satisfied the credit for victory can go nowhere else, God gives Gideon the strategy for battle, and victory is won!

There is more to Gideon's story. He certainly had his issues, but we will end our time with him here with this last thought: it is in our weakness that God's strength is perfected. God will often give us a destiny that seems impossible to humans. He will not share His glory, so He asks us to do what looks impossible to us. I have often asked God to remove my limitations, so I can do more for Him. In reality, the limitations may be His design to ensure the credit for success goes to the right place.

In addition to making sure glory is not misdirected, limitations can bring about creativity. The battle strategy God gave Gideon involved none of his 300 men having a sword. The weapons to be used were trumpets, torches, and empty pitchers. As the saying goes, "necessity is the mother of invention," so instead of fighting against limitations, let's ask God for His ideas and creativity to overcome them for His glory.

For contrast, let's look at the story of someone whom I wouldn't consider one of my heroes. He is listed among the honored in Hebrews 11, and yet, part of his victory was given to someone else. This is the story of Barak, and it takes place during one of the many cycles of Israel's disobedience — oppression, return, and deliverance — in the Old Testament. In fact, Barak served with the judge of Israel immediately preceding Gideon.

We meet Barak in Judges 4 while Israel is being oppressed by a cruel enemy commander named Sisera. Deborah, the prophetess and judge of Israel at the time, calls Barak and says, "God has said you should march to Mount Tabor with 10,000 men from Naphtali and Zebulun. He will bring Sisera and all of his army and deliver them into your hands."

Barak decides he will obey this word, but with a condition — if Deborah will come along, he'll go; if she won't go, neither will he. Deborah agrees to accompany him, but there is a consequence to his bargain. "She said, 'I will surely go with you; nevertheless, the honor shall not be yours on the journey you are about to take, for the Lord will sell Sisera into the hands of a woman.' Then Deborah arose and went with Barak to Kedesh" (Judges 4:9).

And so they go to where the Lord has asked, and He is true to His word. Sisera and his armies and chariots show up, and God delivers every last man into Barak's army's hands — every man, that is, except Sisera, who escapes on foot to the tent of Heber, a friend of Jabin, the king whom Sisera serves.

Heber's wife, Jael, comes out to meet the commander and invites him inside to hide. He accepts the offer of help, and after a short while, finds himself wrapped in a rug with his head nailed to the ground by a tent peg through the temple — though I doubt he was aware of this fact for long. Jael, a housewife in the middle of the desert, had the honor of ridding Israel of this cruel oppressor because of Barak's conditional obedience.

I don't know why Barak required Deborah's presence. If the reason was pure cowardice, I doubt we would see his name among the likes of Abraham, Isaac, Jacob, Joseph, Moses, David, Gideon and others. We are given very little information about him other than this one chapter. He was a great warrior, and God chose Him to deliver Israel from the cruel oppression of King Jabin and his commander.

God will accomplish His purposes, but we can choose whether or not to be a part of the process!

I also don't know why his request for Deborah's presence cost him the honor of killing Sisera himself. If Sisera had not been killed, he would likely have built up another army and continued to oppress Israel. When Barak gave only conditional obedience to God's request, perhaps God understood he could not be trusted to fully complete the task. God will accomplish His purposes, but we can choose whether or not to be a part of the process!

Whatever the reasons for the outcomes in this story, it is a valuable lesson for us to remember as we seek to fulfill our destiny and calling. Thank God He is okay with us asking for confirmations, but be careful about bargaining with God. The biggest difference I see between Gideon and Barak in these stories is that Gideon requested something and Barak demanded.

Another of my favorite people in the Bible is King David. I've already mentioned how much I admire David's openness with God, but there is more to the story. When David's story begins (as far as we know), God is regretting His choice to make Saul king over Israel. He has searched the world, decided on Saul's successor, and sent Samuel to anoint the chosen future king. On seeing the oldest of Jesse's sons, Samuel is convinced he must be the one. Nope! Seven sons later, God has declined each of them, so Samuel is left questioning if there are any other children. So David is summoned from the field where he's been hanging out with the sheep, and we get our first glimpse of the man after God's own heart.

The Bible says he was ruddy, or red, and handsome. I'm not sure about the handsome part because we aren't given much to go on, but I'm not surprised he was red. He had just arrived after running from who knows how far away from where he tended his sheep. Appearances aside, this was the boy God had chosen to one day rule over his people. Samuel anointed him with oil, marking him as the future king, and his journey to the throne began.

> The remarkable thing I notice is that David's identity and purpose are declared long before it is evident to him or anyone else. The first time we see him, he is being anointed as God's chosen leader for His people.

Again, the remarkable thing I notice is that David's identity and purpose are declared long before it is evident to him or anyone else. The first time we see him, he is being anointed as God's chosen leader for His people. Can you imagine how that must have felt? One minute you're hanging out with sheep, the next you're anointed as king, and then the following moment, you're back with the sheep! I'm guessing it's a bit difficult to feel like a king when your only subjects rank among the dumbest animals on the planet.

David's journey to the throne was bumpy, to say the least! David did nothing to bring about the difficulties that awaited him on his way to realizing the destiny of being king of Israel. He served and respected Saul, even when he had the opportunity to hasten his own rise to power. But let's not jump too deeply into his story; I'm getting ahead of myself.

David's first step on the journey to becoming king was a promotion. Instead of caring for and singing to sheep all the time, he now spent some of his time as a musician for a mad king. During the time he was splitting time watching his father's sheep and singing for the man he was destined to replace, he fought with and overcame a lion, a bear, and a giant. With the final victory, David won fame throughout Israel and awakened the jealousy of a king who began to see him as a threat rather than a faithful and valiant servant.

For several years, possibly even a decade or more after he was anointed as the future king of Israel, David continued to serve, and then be hunted by his predecessor. After having a spear hurled at him on two separate occasions, David finally ran for his life. He spent time living in other lands, hiding in caves, and bypassing opportunities to kill Saul and move from the caves to the palace. On two separate occasions, David had Saul in his grasp and was encouraged to strike. He could finally stop running for his right to survive. But both times, he refused to touch the Lord's anointed. Even though he, too, was the Lord's anointed and God's top choice for Saul's job, David would not take a short cut to the end goal.

David knew God was the One who had chosen him, and God must be the One to bring about the fulfillment of his anointing. David's integrity and character were growing through his struggles, and as painful as that decade must have been, he would not hasten the end of the process. I cannot imagine trying to hold onto the identity and destiny of ruling the people of God while hiding in holes and caves simply to survive. It's no wonder he was honest with God; He could trust no one else!

Obviously, David still had faults, and he failed pretty spectacularly in accomplishing some tasks. But he is still the only person in the Bible to be called someone "after God's own heart." He led the people of Israel for nearly 33 years, and then passed the throne on to Solomon, who completed the temple of God and ruled the kingdom with great wisdom — wisdom provided straight from God.

There is so much more to the story of David; however, the part leading up to his reign over Israel is the most fascinating to me. Later in life, he would face similar choices with his son Absalom as he did with King Saul. With the fate of Israel at stake, he had to choose again whether to fight for his place as king or let God decide the outcome. Perhaps my favorite book ever written is called *A Tale of Three Kings*, and it is the story of David and his responses to Saul and Absalom. I have always loved the story of David, but reading *A Tale of Three Kings* brought his story alive in new ways.

The most poignant piece to David's story is the long journey between the first glimpse of his destiny and the fulfillment of it. The same idea is present in different forms in the stories of so many other heroes of the faith. I mentioned Joseph and Moses in an earlier chapter, and they are two that come to mind almost immediately when I think of this common thread: waiting in the wilderness. Joseph's wilderness was slavery and prison. Moses spent 40 years in a literal wilderness. David spent at least part of a decade on the run in the wilderness. These men, and so many other biblical heroes, spent years in the wilderness as they were prepared for their destiny. Gene Edwards, author of *A Tale of Three Kings*, refers to David's wilderness as the "School of Brokenness," and I think that title applies aptly to all of these stories.

I have experienced my own seasons of attending that "school," and I must say, as miserable as the wilderness can be, I would not trade those seasons of my life for anything. As I look back over my life, those times in the School of Brokenness are the times when I grew into the person I am today. One of the greatest things we can learn from those who have gone before us is the value of persevering through the wilderness. God's grace is sufficient, and if we endure and are willing to learn the lessons offered in each course, we will look more like Jesus when we reach graduation!

Many other great stories of identity and destiny abound in the Bible. This chapter would be a book all in its own if I discussed Jacob, Esther, Nehemiah, Peter, Paul, John, and the many others whose stories we could explore. As much as I love all their stories, let's look briefly at one more of my hero's stories: Mary, mother of Jesus.

When we first meet Mary, she is most likely a teenager, and she is betrothed to a young man named Joseph. One day, an angel shows up and announces she is highly favored by God, and He is with her. Only after this declaration of her identity as one of God's favorites does the angel move on to share the purpose for which God has chosen her. Once again, the foundation of purpose seems to flow out of a revelation of identity in relation to God.

> I love Mary's humility and simple obedience at the announcement of her mission. She is told she has been chosen to carry and raise the Son of God. Her immediate response is "Behold, I am a servant of the Lord; let it be to me according to your word."

I love Mary's humility and simple obedience at the announcement of her mission. She is told she has been chosen to carry and raise the Son of God, along with a brief explanation from the angel of how this will happen, even though she is a virgin. Her immediate response is "Behold, I am a servant of the Lord; let it be to me according to your word."

I remember initially thinking Mary had it so good. As a girl who has wanted to be a mother for longer than I can remember, I couldn't imagine having a more wonderful job than being asked to raise a perfect child. I have known parents who believed their child could do no wrong. Sadly, from my experience, the children of such parents are often the nightmare of babysitters everywhere. Imagine actually having a child who never sinned!

Still, I have a feeling when Mary said those words, she didn't fully understand to what she was agreeing. Surely she knew the neighbors would talk, but did she know Joseph would consider a quiet divorce before their marriage had even begun? Of course, she knew she would be raising a son, but did she know enough of the Old Testament prophecies to realize she would also watch him be raised onto a cross? Could she have had any idea the agony her heart would go through watching her firstborn be tortured and die a criminal's death despite his perfect life?

I cannot imagine Mary knew all that was in store as she answered the call of God on her life. I believe many of the others we've talked about, most likely, had no clue the paths they would take to their destinations, of which God had given them only glimpses.

If we view the lives of our predecessors as a picture of our own futures, our lives would end very differently than we've planned. I'm convinced when I make plans, God gets a good chuckle at how small they are. If we are to live up to the calling God has given us, we must be prepared for God to take us into the uncharted waters for a stroll on the waves. Our heroes of the faith were willing to persevere and step out into the unknown because they knew God had chosen them and created them for a purpose. It is no different for us or the generations to come. We are here for a reason, so let's discover it!

QUESTIONS TO PONDER:

1. Who is your favorite person in the Bible?

   _____

   _____

   _____

   _____

   _____

2. Why do you like that person's story? Is there something specific you like?

   _____

   _____

   _____

   _____

   _____

3. Is there a person in the Bible you identify with?

   _____

   _____

   _____

   _____

   _____

4. What can you learn from his or her story?

   _____

   _____

   _____

   _____

   _____

RECOMMENDED LISTENING:

1. "Oceans" by Hillsong United

_____

_____

2. *Music Inspired by The Story* Compilation album

_____

_____

RECOMMENDED READING:

3. Judges 4–9 (Barak & Gideon)

_____

_____

4. 1 Samuel 16–1 Kings 2 (David)

_____

_____

5. The Gospels (Mary, Mother of Jesus)

_____

_____

6. "A Tale of Three Kings" by Gene Edwards

_____

_____

RECOMMENDED VIEWING:

7. The Passion of the Christ (particularly the scenes involving his interactions with his mother)

_____

_____

Part IV: Integration

"The way God designed our bodies is a model for understanding our lives together as a church: every part dependent on every other part, the parts we mention and the parts we don't, the parts we see and the parts we don't. If one part hurts, every other part is involved in the hurt, and in the healing. If one part flourishes, every other part enters into the exuberance. You are Christ's body — that's who you are! You must never forget this. Only as you accept your part of that body does your 'part' mean anything." – 1 Corinthians 12:25–27 (MSG)

LIVE

CHAPTER EIGHTEEN

BELONGING TO THE BODY

"Two are better than one because they have a good return for their labor. For if either of them falls the one will lift up his companion. But woe to the one who falls when there is not another to lift him up... A cord of three strands is not quickly torn apart." – Ecclesiastes 4:9–10, 12

While standing on the shoulders of those who have lived before us may give us insights into the road ahead, they are not the only people in our stories. They aren't even the most important people. Those standing beside us, walking their own journey along this road, are the ones who matter more.

No one is alone in this world, nor should they be. Yet I have been told repeatedly over the years "God is enough." When one laments to another Christian about a state of loneliness, it seems some version of that sentiment is the standard answer to offer "encouragement." But God Himself declared, "It is not good for the man to be alone."

Adam was in the Garden of Eden *with God*, and God still deemed it necessary to make Eve so Adam wouldn't be "alone."

It is true; the fulfillment of our deepest needs and desires to be known, to be loved, and to belong can only fully be filled with God. Any relationship with another person will fall short of true fulfillment if we see them as our only source of meeting the needs of love and belonging. However, we were created in the image of a relational God, and we need relationships with other people in order to thrive. We, those who have accepted the grace of God and relationship with Him, are part of the Church — not the building where weekly meetings take place, but the global family of God the Church is meant to be.

Being the Church

The ministry I work with has been talking in recent years about the numbers of young people leaving the Church. Some of the statistics are deceiving, though. While the people of my generation and younger are leaving the Church in large numbers, they are not all abandoning the Church. Their faith remains intact, along with their desire to serve God and their neighbors.

I will admit I have been tempted at times to join the ranks of those seeking fellowship in a different context than the organized services so many attend each week.[20] Almost without fail, when I mention the temptation, I am directed to Hebrews 10:24–25, which states, "Let us consider how to stimulate one another to love and good deeds, not forsaking our own assembling together, as is the habit of some, but encouraging one another."

---

20 If you have chosen to leave the Church or organized religion because of the problems you see - hypocrisy, fakeness, disunity, judgmental attitudes, etc. - please don't stop having fellowship with other believers. The Church is made up of people who will always have problems and will always disappoint, but the Church is also God's idea. It is His Bride. He loves His Church passionately, and instead of pronouncing judgment that it is no longer worthy of your time, I would urge you to ask God how you can work with Him to bring change in the areas where churches need it most.

I want to emphasize that these words were written to people who didn't meet together once a week, sing a few songs, listen to a sermon, and have surface-level conversation over a cup of coffee afterward. None of these church activities are wrong, but they are not what constitute Church. Check out the description of the early Church in Acts 2:42–47:

"They were continually devoting themselves to the apostles' teaching and to fellowship, to the breaking of bread and to prayer. Everyone kept feeling a sense of awe; and many wonders and signs were taking place through the apostles. And all those who had believed were together and had all things in common; and they began selling their property and possessions and were sharing them with all, as anyone might have need. Day by day continuing with one mind in the temple, and breaking bread from house to house, they were taking their meals together with gladness and sincerity of heart, praising God and having favor with all the people. And the Lord was adding to their number day by day those who were being saved."

> While the people of my generation and younger are leaving the Church in large numbers, they are not all abandoning the Church. Their faith remains intact, along with their desire to serve God and their neighbors.

Does that description fit the place where you gather each week? I'm not saying we have to live all together in a commune or that no one can own property, but a number of the places I have gathered with other believers on a weekly basis looked differently than what is portrayed in Acts. These verses show me authentic community. They ate together, they gave to one another, and they lived out their faith together.

Doing life in community with other believers strips away the ability to pretend all is well. As I mentioned in chapter 4, some people show up to the church building each week and give convincing performances, afraid to show their secret struggles to anyone else. Living life alongside our fellow believers makes it impossible to keep up the façade of perfection we so often want to portray. We can only pretend for so long before the shell cracks and all that is inside spills out. Community brings about the opportunity for "iron to sharpen iron" (Proverbs 27:17).

There is so much we can learn from one another as we walk this journey of life together. I know I need sharpening in areas of my life, and I'm sure there are areas I don't even know about yet which need work. It is through authentic and deep relationships with others that God highlights those places, and He uses people in the process of sharpening me — through prayer, words of correction, wisdom and encouragement.

If I shy away from engaging in deep fellowship with others, I lose out not only on their friendship but the benefits of the sharpening God can do through them. It is often uncomfortable, but that is the model of the early Church; that is the "assembling together and encouraging one another" that I believe the writer of Hebrews was urging us not to forsake.

For those who attend a church with thousands of members, do you disappear and hide in the crowd, or do you engage with others at a deep level and allow them to be a part of your life? Even if you attend a smaller church building, do you slip in just after the service starts and slip out just before you have to actually talk to anyone? If you attend a service without allowing others into your life, I suggest you have already forsaken the point of assembling together.

Attending weekly meetings is good for me and my fellow parishioners. And even when I don't want to attend, I choose to go. Usually, I make that choice because of the people I will meet there. It is about engaging with people in relationships and joining with them in worshiping God. Power lies with believers coming together to worship and seek God. Matthew 18:20 states, "For where two or three have gathered together in my name, I am there in their midst." God inhabits the praises of His people, and when He shows up, the world can be changed.

One other point to note about the passage from Acts is that they had "favor with all the people. And the Lord was adding to their number day by day those who were being saved." Others could see the love they had for God and for one another, and they were drawn into community with them. I love seeing churches that serve their neighbors and show God's love to those outside the walls of the church. Living out our faith in community with other believers and serving on behalf of our neighbors brings favor with people outside the Church.

So many churches are more concerned with their own denomination's distinctive beliefs and traditions that they forget that a belief in Jesus Christ is the common denominator and the foundation for the Church. Peter's declaration that Jesus was the Son of God is the cornerstone on which Christ said He would build His Church. Yes, there are many issues on which churches — and the individuals within them — have differing beliefs, but they are secondary issues.

It doesn't matter what denomination you are, or whether you attend a house church or a church with a massive building and thousands of members. If you believe in Jesus Christ — his miraculous birth, death and resurrection — and have accepted His salvation and surrendered your life to Him, we are related to one another in the family of God, joined together in the Body of Christ.

One Body

We are a part of something much bigger than ourselves, and our part is necessary for the Body to be whole and healthy. I mentioned in Chapter 2 that I enjoyed learning about the human body and how it all works together. A few cells here and there that don't function the way they were designed can cause the entire body to become unhealthy. Every part of the body is needed, and the same goes for each member of Christ's Body. You are important — whether you feel like it or not.

At one of the training schools I was a part of, we had a speaker whose teaching has since had quite an impact in my life. She spoke about asking God what part of the Body you are. It was a simple enough idea. The Bible refers to the Body of Christ in several passages.[21] It says we all have different roles, roles that are equally as important as every other member of the Body. The speaker simply recommended that each person in the class ask God what part He had designed us to be.

To be honest, I didn't get an answer to the question at that time. I did ask the question, but it didn't seem all that important then. The seed had been planted, though. Several years later, it would grow into an important part of my understanding of my purpose, against which I would measure future opportunities.

One morning, during my first trip to Jordan, I was spending time with Jesus, and this concept came to mind again. It had been four years since I first heard the teaching, and I had not really thought about it since. That morning, however, I felt I should ask God what part of the Body I was designed to be. I fully expected the answer to be one of the obvious and visible parts like hands, feet, or mouth.

All my life, I had heard that, as Christians, we needed to be the hands and feet of Jesus to the world, so I assumed those were the standard answers. Instead, the answer I got was "blood vessels." To which I responded, "God, what the heck are you talking about?"

> Every part of the body is needed, and the same goes for each member of Christ's Body. You are important — whether you feel like it or not.

Aside from the impact of what I've learned about my calling through this revelation, my favorite part of telling this story is God's response to my question. "You're a nurse; figure it out," is the reply that sounded loudly in my mind and heart. And so I began to think about the function of the blood vessels in our bodies, which is basically to carry blood. Veins carry blood to the heart, and arteries carry it from the heart to the rest of the body. As I have continued to process this revelation, I feel God said I am an artery.

---

21 Especially Romans 12 and 1 Corinthians 12.

So, what's the deal with arteries? How does knowing they carry blood away from the heart define my function in the Body of Christ? Well, the next thing I thought of was a phrase in the Bible about blood. The phrase appears in several verses; one of which is Deuteronomy 12:23, "for the *blood is* the *life*" (emphasis mine). That's when it hit me; my function in the Body of Christ is to carry life from the heart of God to his Body!

During the years since that first revelation, I have learned more about the privilege and pain of being a conduit for life. When an injury occurs in the body, blood rushes to that area to bring whatever is necessary to heal the wound. If the wound is allowed to bleed freely for a short time, the blood can clean debris out of the wound to prevent festering and infection. However, in order for the blood to flow and bring these benefits, the blood vessels must be broken or pierced right along with the part of the body that is injured. I have the privilege of sharing in the pain of others and ministering to them in the midst of it, but it is not a comfortable privilege.

> When someone in the Church is hurting, it affects everyone around that person. Like it or not, we are connected to the people around us. We are a Body, and we are family — brothers and sisters joined by our Father in heaven.

The discomfort is not limited to blood vessels either; being any part of the Body can be uncomfortable at times. As I write this chapter, I am acutely aware that I slept in the wrong position last night and pinched a nerve in my neck. Not only is my neck sore, but pain is radiating into my left shoulder and all the way down my arm. As stated in 1 Corinthians 12:26, "And if one member suffers, all the members suffer with it." Likewise, when someone in the Church is hurting, it affects everyone around that person. Like it or not, we are connected to the people around us. We are a Body, and we are family — brothers and sisters joined by our Father in heaven.

It is important to know who we are in relation to God, and it is important to know what our purpose is. However, if we try to live out our identity and purpose outside the context of the Church, we are wasting our time and energy. We were made to be in community, and the purpose of the gifts God has placed within us is to *give* them to others. 1 Corinthians 12 discusses the body and the gifts God has given each of us, and then it leads directly into the "love chapter."

Giving & Receiving in Love

1 Corinthians 13 continues the message of chapter 12 by describing the manner in which we use our gifts. Yes, the chapters are talking about the gifts of the Spirit — prophecy, healing, tongues, wisdom, knowledge, to name a few — but I think the principle holds true for all of the talents and gifts God has put into each one of us. Unless we are using our gifts in love, for our friends and neighbors, they are just a bunch of racket. In short, we are missing the purpose of our gifts and our lives if we are not using them on behalf of other people, whether they are a part of the Body of Christ or not. We are blessed to be a blessing to others.

As important as this is, it is also important to receive from other people. Sometimes, accepting help is more difficult than offering it. I live on financial support from people who want to be a part of what God has called me to do. Even after more than a decade, I often find it difficult to accept money and simply say thank you. What I have learned, though, is the people who offer me their support — not only financial but also prayers, encouragement, and even correction — receive a blessing, too. They share in the fruit that is produced through the work they are supporting. We are all in this together.

As we seek to live our lives in intimacy with God, we must allow people to be an integral part of our lives as well. It is always a risk to engage deeply with others because unlike God, they will fail us. However, without them, our identity and the intentions God has for our lives will never be realized. The Body of Christ needs us to do our part, and that can only happen if we remain within and connected closely to the rest of the Body.

QUESTIONS TO PONDER:

1. Do you have deep relationships with other believers? Do you have people you trust to "sharpen" you and who will allow you to "sharpen" them?

   _____

   _____

   _____

   _____

   _____

2. Have you been tempted to abandon the Church? Why or why not?

   _____

   _____

   _____

   _____

   _____

3. Does your church have problems? How can you partner with God to see His best done with those problems?

   _____

   _____

   _____

   _____

RECOMMENDED READING:

1. Romans 12, 1 Corinthians 12–13

   _____

   _____

CHAPTER NINETEEN

A JOURNEY OF DISCOVERY

"It is our choices, Harry, that show what we truly are, far more than our abilities." – J.K. Rowling, *Harry Potter & the Chamber of Secrets*

Well, friend, we've nearly reached the end of this book, but our journey is just beginning. Thankfully, God will continue to lead each of us along the path. We may not see the final destination, or even the next step, but the mystery doesn't have to bring fear. I mentioned in the introduction that our search for our true identity doesn't have to be a crisis. We can cease striving and simply take each step as God reveals it to us. Our identity and our purpose are comprised of many aspects. As we are faithful to seek God, He will reveal these aspects to us in the ways and times He chooses.

As I shared in the preceding chapter, through asking God the simple question of what part of the Body I am, I have learned much about

179

my purpose. I am called to minister to the Body. This doesn't mean I shouldn't be involved in sharing God's love with the people who don't know Him already. However, just like Paul knew his calling was to share the gospel with the Gentiles, I know my calling is to bring life and healing to the Body so it can be effective in its functions. The outworking of that may look differently in the coming seasons of my life, but that is my purpose in life.

One of the things I find most interesting in the story of discovering my function in the Body of Christ is the timing. Why did God wait four years to answer my Body part question? Looking back now, I realize I wasn't ready to understand the answer until I understood more of my own identity (mainly through the story of Éowyn, as I've shared in Part Two of this book). That realization is another reminder of the importance of knowing and accepting my identity in order to be able to move into my purpose. "I will be a healer, and love all things that grow and are not barren."

> As we go deeper in our relationship with God and learn more and more about the identity God has given us, we have the choice to move forward into our purpose or to hide from it.

As we go deeper in our relationship with God and learn more and more about the identity God has given us, we have the choice to move forward into our purpose or to hide from it. Like Dumbledore told Harry Potter in the opening quote of this chapter, it is largely our choices that show who we are. It is very likely many others missed being listed among the heroes of the faith in Hebrews chapter 11 because they chose to yield to fear instead of accepting and living out the identity God spoke over them.

While our choices are a significant factor in knowing who we are, it does not mean our abilities have nothing to do with discovering and living out our destiny. God has given each of us gifts and passions, and He intends for us to use them and enjoy them. For some passions, extra training may be needed, and for others, maybe not so much.

A number of years ago, I seriously considered returning to school to get a Master's degree in counseling. I realized that while I was drawn to nursing as a way to gain access to countries that don't welcome missionaries, it is not a profession that I enjoyed. My favorite class in nursing school was mental health, and for years, I have been drawn to counseling.

As I prayed more about it, though, I realized that what I am drawn to is bringing healing. There is a place for trained counselors and medical professionals, but that is not primarily what God has called me to be. I constantly have friends coming to me to process information, to receive prayer, or to get advice. But mostly, they need me just to listen. For me, I realized a degree would just be a piece of paper to prove to myself who I already am.

Don't hear me wrong! I do not consider myself a counselor, and I don't present myself to others as one. I tell people to seek a counselor if that's what they need. The people who come to me are usually just in need of someone to listen and ask the right questions while they arrive at their own answers. That is something God has given me the ability and wisdom to do. He has also given me a passion and love for people; therefore, people know I truly care about them when they share with me, even if I'm asking tough questions or challenging them. He has given me a passion for this message of identity and purpose and the courage to share it through this book.

The stories throughout this book are just glimpses of the process I have been through over the past several years as I have come to know who I am and why I'm here. I guarantee your process will look differently. Thank you for walking this far with me and reading my story. I hope it has been enjoyable, but mostly, I hope it has helped you to see that you matter because God made you and chose you! You are on earth for a purpose and your Maker/Lover (and everything in between) has designed you especially for the incredible destiny He has in store for you. As we finish this part of our journey together, I want to pray and then leave you with some questions to get you thinking and moving along your path with Jesus.

Dear God,

Thank You for choosing to create us. Thank You for making each of us in Your image, and yet also unique. Thank You for sending Jesus as the sacrifice to bridge the gap we created through our selfishness. Thank You for the protection and provision You offer and for the words of life You speak to us. Thank You for the chance to serve You and the people around us, and for the privilege of being Your friends. Thank You for adopting each of us into Your family and being a good Father to us. And finally, thank You for loving us in a way that is beyond what we can comprehend. Thank You for choosing each of us as Your Beloved and making a way for us to choose You in return.

Thank You for the identity You have put into each one of us. I ask that as we seek You, You show each of us more and more of the person You had in mind when You knit us together. Help us to always keep the focus on You and not to lose ourselves in the search for our destiny. Help us to see everyday opportunities as a chance to walk in our understanding of who we are in You and to walk courageously into those opportunities. Illuminate lies we believe about ourselves, and as we repent of those lies, fill us with Your truth instead.

Thank You for the destiny and purpose You intended for each of us when you designed us. Guide us to passions, skills, and callings You have for each of us. Build up our character so we can be successful in the things You call us to do and give us the grace to go through each season of our lives. Help us to live always mindful of the Kingdom You are building and to seek ways that we can partner with You in bringing Your Kingdom to earth. Grow our passion to partner with You through prayer and action to see Your will be done on earth as it is in Heaven.

Thank You for the stories of the heroes of the faith, both in the Bible and those who have lived since the Bible was written. Thank You for using seemingly ordinary people like us to do extraordinary things for You. Thank You for the opportunity to learn from those who've gone before us on this journey. As we continue the journey and live our own part in Your story, help us to be mindful of those who may one day gain courage and insights from our stories. Bring people alongside us to sharpen us and make us more like You, and show us ways to encourage and sharpen those You put in our lives each day. Give us a passion for Your Body, and help each of us to fulfill our part in the Body.

I pray now for each person who is seeking You for their own identity and purpose. Guide each of them on the path that leads first to Your glory and then to fulfillment in their lives!

In Jesus Name, Amen.

Now, get ready to take notes and be ready for God to reveal remarkable insights, both now and in the future! Remember, this is a process.

Questions to ask others — choose carefully the people who will answer seriously, thoughtfully, and truthfully.

1. What 3–5 words or phrases would you use to describe me?

2. What do you see that I am good at?

3. What occupation do you think I would be good at?

4. Have you noticed anything that brings me to life or excites me?

5. Which Bible character would you compare me to? Which fictional character? Why?

Questions to ask yourself

1. Where am I in my relationship with God? Have I accepted Him as my Father and the Lover of my Soul?

2. What has He said about me so far?

3. Which Bible character do I most identify with? Which fictional character? Why?

4. What am I passionate about?

5. What do I enjoy?

6. What special skills and abilities do I have? (Be honest, and don't sell yourself short! You have special skills.)

7. As a child, what did I want to be when I grew up? Were there answers that came up repeatedly or that were always on the list?

8.   Who are the people I like working with; is there a certain age or group of people I am drawn to?

9.   What issues, needs or ministries concern or excite me most?

10.   If there were no limits to where I could go and what I could do with my life, what would my dream be?

Questions to ask God

1.   What do you see when you look at me?

2.   Which facets of your image and character am I meant to display to others?

3.   Ho do I bring you the most pleasure? The most glory?

4.   What is my original design? What did you create me for?

5.   How can I live out my destiny in the place I'm in today? How am I already living it out? What practical steps can I take to move in that direction?

6.   Which part of the Body am I? What is my function?

7.   Which experiences in my life do you want to use and how?

QUESTIONS TO PONDER:

1. What have you learned about God?

_____

_____

_____

_____

_____

_____

_____

2. What have you learned about yourself?

_____

_____

_____

_____

_____

_____

_____

3. Are you aware of any new dreams in your heart for the future?

_____

_____

_____

_____

_____

_____

_____

RECOMMENDED ACTIVITIES:

1. Take time to truly listen to and communicate with God. **Don't get discouraged if you don't receive immediate answers. I didn't get an answer about which part of the Body I am until four years after I asked the first time.

_____

_____

_____

_____

_____

2. Find a person you trust with whom to share your thoughts. It is good to be wise about whom you share with, but choose someone you can talk to and who will encourage you and challenge you in the things you are learning about God, yourself and your destiny.

_____

_____

_____

_____

_____

3. Keep a written record of what you discover. When lies come to mind, you will be able to combat them with declarations of the truth.

_____

_____

_____

_____

_____

_____

Lightning Source UK Ltd.
Milton Keynes UK
UKOW06f0209100916

282613UK00002B/123/P